A:shiwi A:wan Ulohnanne
The Zuni World

Jim Enote and Jennifer McLerran, Editors

A:shiwi A:wan Museum
& Heritage Center

MUSEUM of
NORTHERN ARIZONA

A:shiwi A:wan Ulohnanne • The Zuni World

Director's Message

Robert G. Breunig, Director, Museum of Northern Arizona

On the opening morning of each of the past three Zuni Festivals held at the Museum of Northern Arizona (MNA) in Flagstaff, there has been a flag raising. The American flag, followed by the flag of the Pueblo of Zuni, have risen together to fly over the canyon of the Rio de Flag at the entrance of the museum. As the flags have ascended, the Zuni Band has played the "Star Spangled Banner." This flag raising is a show of American patriotism at the beginning of the Memorial Day holiday, for fallen American veterans, including Zuni veterans. However, for the Zunis, it is more. Seeing their flag flying here is a palpable reminder that this land—the land surrounding the sacred mountain that they call Sunha:kwin K'yaba:chu Yalanne and the Euro-Americans call the San Francisco Peaks—was part of Zuni traditional territory.

Zuni flag raising ceremony at the Museum of Northern Arizona. Photograph by Michele Mountain, MNA.

In a historical, cultural, and spiritual sense, this is still their land. Indeed, much of what we call the Colorado Plateau today is traditional Zuni territory. From their origin place in the Grand Canyon, the ancestors of the Zuni moved through time over much of the Plateau. Over millennia, they migrated up drainages, over mountain ranges, and through major river valleys, until they found the Middle Place, the place where they are today centered physically, psychologically, and spiritually, at Zuni Pueblo or Halona: Idiwana'a. Yet even though they settled in what is now New Mexico, they did not give up their connections to those places where they had once lived, connections that they still maintain today.

Director's Message

The present Zuni Reservation is a fraction of their old territory, and led to their being defined as a "New Mexico tribe." As Zunis sought to have a voice in issues affecting places outside New Mexico, including the Grand Canyon in Arizona, their standing was questioned: "But you're a New Mexico tribe," they heard. A map, and a state line, had defined their status on many issues of importance to them. This exhibit of Zuni Map Art challenges these inaccurate assumptions.

With the revival of the Zuni Festival at the Museum of Northern Arizona in 2008, MNA entered into a partnership with the A:shiwi A:wan Museum and Heritage Center as a festival co-sponsor. This partnership signaled wide-ranging collaborations between the two museums. One of the explicit goals of the A:shiwi A:wan Museum and Heritage Center was to instill in the public an awareness of the Zuni traditional cultural landscape and their ongoing interest in these lands.

The exhibit, *A:shiwi A:wan Ulohnanne - The Zuni World*, displays the works of the Zuni Map Art project, another manifestation of this interest in traditional Zuni lands. The A:shiwi A:wan Museum staff has, through this project, raised awareness within the Zuni community of their traditional lands and has provided each Zuni household with some of these images in poster form. This exhibit takes their initiative to a wider audience. Through the paintings displayed in the exhibit and published in this catalog, Zuni artists are showing us how they see their own history, their ancestral migrations, their ancient homes, and their places of cultural significance.

All of us at the Museum of Northern Arizona are proud to be a part of this culturally significant initiative.

A:shiwi on A:shiwi
Zuni on Zuni

Jim Enote

We cannot draw a line around the Zuni world. It would be as impossible as declaring the end of art.

The Zuni have always had maps. We have maps in songs and prayers, painted on ceramics, and etched in stone. Our maps aid our memories, they give reference to our places of origin, places we have visited, and places we hope to go. They also provide us with a reference of where we are within the universe and help to define our relationship to natural processes surrounding us. And because these maps are ours, they function within our particular cultural sensibilities.

But over the past 500 years we have been remapped. Our names of places and their meanings have been all but eliminated from mainstream use. In their place we've been given a new set of maps, with a new set of names that reflect other values and ways of seeing the world that has been our home for generations. Chimik'yana'kya is now called the Grand Canyon, Sunha:kwin K'yaba:chu Yalanne are now the San Francisco Peaks, Ts'u'yal'a are shown as the Sangre de Cristo Mountains above Santa Fe, and the list goes on. For many Zuni, these names are foreign and disorienting. In some cases they are also a direct denial of our history and our presence on the land, for along with the new names and new maps came new assumed ownerships and control of our territories and resources.

Before serving as Director of the A:shiwi A:wan Museum, I was co-director of the Indigenous Communities Mapping Initiative, providing mapping assistance to indigenous communities in North America and Hawaii. It was during that work that I saw an immense movement among indigenous communities to create maps using computers. I recognize computerized maps are very practical and are a standard within and across many professions. If I ever needed to provide a map in court, in addition to drawing one myself I would probably produce computerized maps because they are so commonly recognized in legal proceedings. But I wonder if computerized mapping and mapping offices could sometimes create unintended gatekeepers for a community's geographic knowledge. What if a map's audience is not familiar with all the lines, numbers, and orientations of computer-generated maps? As an artist, albeit an interrupted one, I knew there must be another way to dignify and represent our mother earth.

After I came to the A:shiwi A:wan Museum, it became clear to me that even though I am Zuni my knowledge of Zuni place names and locations was incomplete, and many other Zunis were in the same predicament. I know from experience it can be embarrassing, or worse humiliating, when you aren't familiar with the places you are singing or praying about. I also know some families are single parent families, and some may have lost members that could share or pass on this sort of knowledge. For many of us, pieces of Zuni culture were missing, and for a variety of reasons we were unable to find a suitable source to understand our cultural landscape.

We Are of This Place

The Zuni community is arguably one of the world's great centers of art. At least one person in practically every household is actively and consistently creating art. In what some might consider a dry and dreary environment, we embellish and embroider the simplest things. We enjoy the sound, look, and feel of beautiful things, and we try to look our best especially during many social and ceremonial events that occur throughout the year.

So it would make sense to say art is a Zuni common denominator. If that is the case, why not make maps in a way that inserts Zuni artists into the mapping process? And to assure that Zuni cultural sensitivities are addressed, why not include cultural advisors as well? In 1996 twelve Zuni advisors gathered at the A:shiwi A:wan Museum to resolve how artists and cultural advisors could make maps that would serve as learning tools for the Zuni community. At the front of these discussions was what *not* to map. Zuni religious knowledge, including some place name knowledge, is not open or accessible to everyone, even at Zuni. Access to such knowledge is partitioned by gender, initiation, and other special circumstances. Only certain Zuni religious groups or individuals know the locations of some sacred sites, and we certainly would not describe these places in our maps. Revealing these places would go against Zuni rules of religious confidentiality and discretion and would doom our work, not to mention our reputations.

After nearly a year of conversation and negotiation, the advisors decided the first three maps would depict the Zuni Village, Zuni Reservation, and general Zuni region. The maps were commissioned through a process that included a request for proposals that went to all known Zuni two-dimensional artists. As part of the proposals, pencil sketches were also requested from the vying artists, to see if they could create maps that would be unconventional and conceptual, and with enough realism to be recognizable. Based on their artistic abilities, understanding of the concept of map art, and willingness to work with advisors, Geddy Epaloose, Ronnie Cachini, and Edward Wemytewa were chosen to create the village, reservation, and regional maps, respectively. This basic process for selecting artists was used as the map art movement continued with new maps and new artists. The first three maps were spectacular and made a huge impact on the people who saw them. We had never seen maps of our lands like these before. These beautiful maps portrayed areas the advisors believed all Zunis should know about and did so without revealing culturally sensitive locations.

We were so inspired by these maps we decided to make posters of them with place names printed over important sites. But we soon learned that each map could potentially include hundreds of places to label. How could we reproduce the beautiful maps as posters without making the maps too busy with text and compromising the art? The advisors solved the problem by selecting only a limited number of places to be labeled. Spelling the place names raised another dilemma. Until only recently Zuni had no written script. Today the international phonetic alphabet is used to create a Romanized script of Zuni words, but the list of spelled words is limited. In the process of labeling sites for the posters, several place names were written for the first time, leading the advisors to stress the importance of pronouncing and spelling the places correctly. One of the advisors, Wilfred Eriacho, a retired Zuni language educator, prepared correct spellings for each labeled site. With place names completed, the posters were printed and given away free to Zuni households, school classrooms, and tribal programs.

The maps were so popular a second series was commissioned depicting Bandelier National Monument, the Four Corners area, the Grand Canyon, and Journey of Zuni Ancestors to the Land of Everlasting Summer. This was followed by a third series representing a theme of water and waterways on the Colorado Plateau. A fourth series details the Zuni relationship to the Grand Canyon, and the fifth renders the fantastic sites known to most people as Chaco Canyon and Mesa Verde.

The artists represented in these works are a who's who of Zuni painters and include a nineteen-year-old emerging artist and some established "masters" in their sixties and seventies. Two women, Mallery Quetawki and Ermalinda Pooacha-Eli, are represented in this collection as well. Both are talented artists who work in a variety of media. They bring a thoughtful woman's view to the collection and have several on-going projects that we will learn more about in the near future. While clearly demonstrating their artistic styles on paper or canvas, these artists in interviews with Jennifer McLerran describe here, in their own words, how they were inspired to make their art and what they came away with as participants in the map art movement.

Interestingly, many of the artists had never been to the most distant places they were commissioned to paint, and consequently they and the cultural advisors journeyed to the areas together so the artists could observe and explore the sites while being informed of the roles the sites play in Zuni history. On a couple of occasions an airplane was hired to take artists to areas difficult to access so they could see the sites from the air and experiment with perspective and landscape textures in their paintings. Levon Loncassion's watercolor, Tribes of the Rio Grande; Geddy Epaloose's Middle Place; and Edward Wemytewa's Waterways are examples of paintings completed with the help of aerial vantages.

Accelerating a Movement

The A:shiwi A:wan Museum and Heritage Center's map art collection is helping to accelerate a movement in art as well as a movement to reverse distortions of our history. It is a movement that is at times slow and halting, a movement that faces political, cultural, and economic obstacles. But it has begun.

The Zuni map art concept asserts that mapping is not limited to technicians. The art is distinctly Zuni and is consistent with Zuni abstraction of nature and its arrangement. The art also mirrors the way we compartmentalize knowledge and represent complex relationships. And these maps are like relatives, like aunts and uncles that entrance us with narrations of places they have been to or heard about. This art holds something that transcends Western modernism and speaks to our own continuous search for the essence of Zuni.

The map artists and advisors are advancing an idea that carefully created maps will help our people understand where we came from and why our culture is associated with places far away from our reservation circumstance. And we can do this in a pleasing way, on our own terms, using our language and Zuni aesthetic sensibilities.

The map art process has enabled Zuni artists and advisors to retrace the footsteps of our ancestors. Within the experience, we shared and cultivated a phenomenal spirit of experimentation and collaboration. These maps are intended for a Zuni audience, but as the advisors have pointed out, the maps are also strategic and therefore can serve a powerful role to inspire non-Zuni audiences and awaken awareness of Zuni perspectives. As tools that help set the record straight, we see these maps as a means to mutual understanding and peace making; the spaces between metaphorical lines, between paintings, and between narratives are spaces for opportunity and performance. I believe these maps will lead to new understandings either by formal agreements or simple appreciation of a Zuni worldview.

And these maps are like relatives, like aunts and uncles that entrance us with narrations of places they have been to or heard about.

The rest of the world may still want their conventional maps, but to evolve as a global society we need to challenge what is conventional and legitimate. We also need to challenge standards and notions that tell us what a map should be.

I believe careless maps are a defeat for everyone. Perhaps native people have been the first to accept the price of careless maps. If that is so, Zuni artists are in a unique position to respond. Essentially, Zuni map art is a collective, revisionist effort to elaborate Zuni history and cultural survival independent from the non-Zuni narrative, and do so in a lovely and appropriate way.

Jim Enote is the Director of the A:shiwi A:wan Museum and Heritage Center at Zuni, New Mexico.

Zuni artists and cultural advisors at Ribbon Falls. Photograph by Jim Enote.

Mapping Memory

Jennifer McLerran

In "Landscape, History and the Pueblo Imagination" Laguna storyteller Leslie Marmon Silko speaks of the importance of oral narratives in Pueblo cultures. Functioning as "maps" to navigate the physical and cultural world and facilitate intimate knowledge of one's surroundings, oral narratives bind communities together and perpetuate their survival. Even something as seemingly mundane as a hunting story, recounting the path followed and the landmarks encountered during the pursuit of game animals, serves as a survival tool for Pueblo community members. Silko explains that "lost travelers, and lost piñon-nut gatherers, have been saved by sighting a rock formation they recognize only because they once heard a hunting story describing this rock formation."[1]

..."lost travelers, and lost piñon-nut gatherers, have been saved by sighting a rock formation they recognize only because they once heard a hunting story describing this rock formation."

While a hunting story may help to ensure physical welfare, more esoteric Pueblo religious knowledge, likewise conveyed orally, works to perpetuate the spiritual vitality of the group. Possessed by select community members and conveyed in a circumscribed fashion, such knowledge is deeply embedded and inextricably intertwined with the places where people have lived and the lands they have repeatedly traversed over many centuries. Like the hunting stories Silko describes, such narratives serve as maps, conveying important information necessary to negotiate a world deeply inflected with spiritual and historical significance.

Community members must maintain close contact if they are to benefit from the experience of others in their group, since only those privy to the knowledge passed on by word of mouth, from person to person, may fully benefit. In traditional cultures such as those of the Pueblos, where important knowledge and lessons are conveyed orally instead of in written form, mechanisms for perpetuating person-to-person transmission have developed and persisted. However, with changes brought by Euro-American contact and subsequent

Zuni Emergence and Migration Mural at the A:shiwi A:wan Museum and Heritage Center. Photograph by Jim Enote.

attrition of some traditional practices and lifeways, Pueblo communities like Zuni have struggled to maintain community cohesion. Educational and economic opportunities often cause tribal members to leave the community for extended periods, and lines of communication and person-to-person contact are strained. This has resulted in development of new and innovative ways to facilitate the communication of important cultural history and religious beliefs.

As Zuni religious leader and jeweler/lapidarist Octavius Seowtewa notes, many individuals in the Zuni community have not been privy to important basic cultural information. Realizing this, Seowtewa and other community members have come together to remedy this problem. As Octavius Seowtewa explains, "Our oral history is very complex." For example, the Zuni Emergence narrative is a two-day recitation that must be passed on to younger family members if it is to survive. In some cases, oral histories are successfully conveyed; however, in others their transmission has been incomplete: "There was this one family that their grandfather knew it from start to finish, and there's two grandsons that he was giving that information to, and I'm not sure if they grasped the whole complex of that recitation. But, at least it's still there, and it's passed on from generation to generation."

Additionally, many community members, because of their particular family situation, have had little exposure to such narratives: "Information is very vague—like I mentioned, from house to house, household to household—if you had a grandfather that at least knew 75 percent or 50 percent, you had some of that information,"

Seowtewa says. Without firsthand experience of the ways in which these crucial cultural narratives connect with the Zuni ancestral lands, a deeper and more nuanced understanding of them escapes younger generations, who must be relied upon to carry them forward.

Octavius Seowtewa explains further that these oral narratives are deeply embedded in a cultural landscape, portions of which the Zuni have been denied access to by processes of colonialism. Subsequent to the appropriation of traditional Zuni lands, the full significance and cultural value of many of these narratives has become remote and—like the landscapes they inscribe—inaccessible. However, with the development of partnerships with the National Park Service and other federal and state entities over the past twenty years, Zuni entities such as the Zuni Cultural Research Advisory Team (ZCRAT), the Zuni Heritage and Historic Preservation Office, and the A:shiwi A:wan Museum and Heritage Center (AAMHC) have facilitated greater access to ancestral sites in previously restricted areas of national parks and other government-supervised areas. In his role as a member of ZCRAT, Seowtewa has made fourteen trips within the Grand Canyon. He explains: "So, every time I make a trip, I'm gathering new information that can be used. . . . With this type of information that we have, we're opening a whole new door for our kids and their grandkids. And, so, that information will be out there for them." This will enable them to continue the project that he and others have started. "We are," says Seowtewa, "connecting some of the dots to our oral history with these places. . . . We never had books about where our ancestors traveled, but they left the marks there to—for future generations—to tie themselves back into these same sites that our ancestors used. And it's like a book. . . that they left behind to tell us 'Yes, we were here, and your people are part of this area'. . . . It just makes our oral history, our migration history, that much more solid. It gives it more depth because we have this information that was left behind, and we're utilizing all that information." With renewed knowledge, he notes, "maybe we can start where we left off and complete the whole history."[2]

Realizing the potential that renewed access to these sites offers, Seowtewa joined a project initiated by Jim Enote, Director of the A:shiwi A:wan Museum and Heritage Center at Zuni. Zuni Map Art has proven to be an effective means of recording and conveying to community members the important cultural history and beliefs embedded in Zuni ancestral lands. The ongoing project, which has grown over the past three years to include sixteen Zuni artists, has brought some of the community's most creative minds together with religious and other community leaders to harness the capacity of visual art to communicate in accessible fashion the importance of the Zuni cultural landscape in perpetuation of community vitality and values.

Varied visual means of encoding and conveying cultural information—both religious and secular—have survived and continue to flourish at Zuni. Zuni Map Art builds on the talent and experience of local visual artists, drawing on the community's long traditions of both secular and sacred painting. Yet the artwork produced as part of this project differs from past Zuni painting in significant ways. Before Euro-American contact, Zuni painting was similar to that of other Pueblo groups. Kiva murals, ceramic decoration, and altar painting were its primary forms.[3] The development of fine art painting as a form of modern expression among Southwest Native Americans in the early- to mid-twentieth century, most notably through the influence of Santa Fe Indian School art teacher Dorothy Dunn, resulted in significant changes in the work of many Pueblo artists.[4] But relatively few Zunis attended the Santa Fe Indian School and so the Studio Style of painting did not have such an impact on the Zuni community. Percy Tsisete Sandy, who attended the Santa Fe Indian School for one year, is a notable exception. While Sandy undoubtedly influenced some Zuni artists, he was married to a Taos Pueblo woman and lived primarily at Taos, so his impact on artists in his community of origin was relatively small.[5]

Another influence on the development of a modern painting tradition at Zuni has been the community's restriction on the representation of religious activities, a prohibition that predominated until quite recently and remains in force to some extent today.[6] Even though many community members frowned on the practice, some early- to mid-twentieth-century Zuni artists did produce work with ceremonial subjects. Among them were brothers Anthony and Theodore Edaakie.[7] Anthony Edaakie is best known for the Shalako murals he produced for long-time Zuni trader C. G. Wallace's dining room at the De Anza Motor Lodge in Albuquerque. A Shriner, Wallace built a "secret" dining room in the motel's basement and commissioned Edaakie to execute the murals.[8] Both Anthony and Theodore also produced numerous paintings, often of ceremonial subjects, that now reside in museum collections, including the Museum of Northern Arizona in Flagstaff, Arizona, and the Indian Art Research Center of the School for Advanced Research in Santa Fe, New Mexico.

Another was Patone (or Charley) Chuyati, whose work is also found in numerous museum collections. Chuyati is best known in the Zuni community for the ceiling murals he painted for the rectory of St. Anthony's Indian School at Zuni in 1929. Commissioned by Father Arno of St. Anthony's, they depict Francisco Coronado and the Spanish priest Fray Marcos de Niza approaching the Zuni village of Hawikku.[9]

Of significant influence on young Zuni artists of the 1920s through the 1950s was teacher Clara Gonzales at the Zuni Day School. Rather than encouraging a romanticized, faux primitive style as prescribed by Dunn at the Santa Fe Indian

Naming of the Clans, Zuni Emergence and Migration Mural at the A:shiwi A:wan Museum and Heritage Center. Photograph by Jim Enote.

School, Gonzales encouraged her students to embrace a modern, realistic style of representation. Also in contrast to Dunn, Gonzales urged her students to represent community members in contemporary dress engaged in the tasks of daily life and to eschew depictions of traditional dress, traditional ceremonial practice, and other religious subjects.

As a result, a distinctive style of modern fine art painting has developed at Zuni Pueblo that is quite different from that which has become commonly identified as twentieth-century Southwest Native American. While the style for which Zuni artists have become known uniquely reflects traditional Zuni conventions, it partakes of modern Western conventions of representation. The decorative flatness of Santa Fe Indian School painting gives way to volumetric forms; and non-perspectival rendering yields to foreshortening and illusionistic representation of deep space. Figures are positioned in fully rendered environments rather than suspended in an idealized and timeless space.

Among the best known and most highly regarded painters at Zuni today are Alex Seowtewa and Duane Dishta. Son of Patone Chuyati, Alex Seowtewa began a series of murals in 1970 depicting the community's traditional ceremonies at Our Lady of Guadalupe Mission Church. He did this at the urging of his father and with the blessing of church authorities.[10] Assisted by his sons Gerald, Kenneth, and Edwin, Seowtewa has continued to work on the murals for nearly forty years, garnering worldwide acclaim. Artist Duane Dishta has gained wide popularity both in the Zuni community and in the wider Native American Art market. Dishta's paintings of Zuni kachinas are found in many Zuni homes and can be obtained through local trading posts and galleries nationwide.

Interviews with artists participating in Zuni Map Art have revealed that Dishta and Alex Seowtewa serve as important exemplars for the younger artists. Also repeatedly cited as influential is Zuni High School art teacher Herrin Othole. His instruction constitutes another important factor in the development of a consistency of style and technique in the work of younger Zuni painters.

While established Zuni artists and local educators have influenced the style of those participating in Zuni Map Art, responsibility for the conceptual basis of the undertaking lies with AAMHC Director and Zuni Map Art Director Jim Enote. A co-founder of the AAMHC, Enote has played an important role in helping to perpetuate painting as an important form of expression at Zuni. Following the ecomuseum model that has provided a new paradigm for cultural preservation efforts in indigenous communities worldwide, the A:shiwi A:wan Museum and Heritage Center focuses on community-based cultural preservation projects.[11] Founded in 1992 by a group of five Zuni tribal members and possessing an all-Zuni staff, the museum's mission is to provide exhibits and programs for the Zuni community that reflect and propagate the

The People Divide Into Three Groups, Zuni Emergence and Migration Mural at the A:shiwi A:wan Museum and Heritage Center. Photograph by Jim Enote.

cultural and environmental values of its people. The AAMHC features a long-term loan exhibit, "Hawikku: Echoes from Our Past," comprised of 221 objects selected by its staff and other Zuni community members from the collections of the Smithsonian Institution. Community programming includes "Pathways to Zuni Wisdom," a series of presentations and field trips that expose Zuni children to traditional knowledge and cultural practices in after-school and summer sessions; "Creating Collaborative Catalogs," which brings Zuni collections housed in distant facilities to Zuni through a database at AAMHC and enables Zuni community members to research and develop a new version of museum catalog; and "Emergence and Migration Mural Presentations," consisting of Zuni oral history presentations to local school groups and other interested parties by AAMHC staff member Curtis Quam using the museum's murals depicting the Zuni peoples' emergence and migration to their current location.

Zuni Map Art is perhaps the AAMHC's most ambitious and far-reaching undertaking to date. Artists have been commissioned to travel to ancestral sites and then, with the aid of a group of community advisors, record the cultural landscapes visited in paintings intended to serve as maps for other community members. The paintings reproduced in this volume display the results so far.

According to Enote, participants believe their map art "can appeal to a global audience and persuade people to consider looking at the world as a cultural landscape rather than only a physical entity."[12] Enote further explains that "in the face of modernity and globalization, Zunis along with other indigenous peoples are struggling to maintain a relationship with cultural landscapes through our aboriginal territories. . . . We believe . . . map art can create new pathways for envisioning, sensing, and respecting our cultural landscapes."

Zuni Map Art is an indigenous community's attempt to stave off cultural degradation in the face of seemingly overwhelming forces. Works produced by artists participating in this project represent various sites in the Grand Canyon and throughout the Colorado Plateau as sacred landscapes while, in Enote's words, "evoking a deeper understanding of our perspective of life sustaining natural features of the Colorado Plateau." Zuni Map Art is a project of cultural survivance as much as an attempt to build community. As archaeologist Peter Whitridge explains in his study of cultural landscapes and the Inuit, such place-making projects serve as means by which "topography is made intelligible and mapped into memory through its articulation with a store of cultural knowledge, and at the same time the community comes into being through the enculturation of individuals to a local history embedded in places."[13] Zuni Map Art works similarly, providing an alternative model for representing the physical world that participates in and reinforces a uniquely Zuni cultural imaginary. This, in turn, reinforces and perpetuates a place-based community identity.[14]

Maps help us navigate our way through the physical world. They encode existing knowledge about the land and the human settlements that occupy it, guiding those unfamiliar with the places they represent. Zuni Map Art similarly encodes knowledge about the land. But, rather than simply guiding passage through the physical world, these maps/paintings provide Zuni community members with aids for navigating through a more hybrid space—one that evidences a belief and a cultural praxis that regards the natural and cultural as complexly intertwined and indistinct. Zuni Map Art encodes cultural memory, providing mnemonic devices for recollecting important connections of land to culture. For those Zuni community members not privy to traditional knowledge handed down from elders, it serves as a means of initiation into traditional knowledge and community history.

Relación Geográficas Map of Cempoala [Zempoala], 1580, 81 x 66.5 cm. Photograph courtesy of the Nettie Lee Benson Latin American Collection, University of Texas Libraries, The University of Texas at Austin (JGI XXV-10).

Zuni lands have, of course, been previously mapped, but from a viewpoint not informed by traditional Zuni knowledge and worldview. For the traditional Zuni, much like the Apache community members with whom anthropologist Keith Basso has worked, cultural knowledge—or wisdom, as Basso describes it—"sits in places."[15] Western mapping practices provide limited means for conveying these insights. As cultural constructs unique to time and place—and thus themselves reflective of important culturally specific beliefs and values—modern Western maps fall short in representing the place-based knowledge that Basso's Native consultants describe.

Indigenous mapping practices are diverse. Examples include Micronesian shell and stick maps which feature shells representing land masses and sticks positioned so as to represent ocean currents, and Inuit wooden maps that serve as tactile guides to those navigating Greenland's coastal waters. Such examples of indigenous mapping traditions provide effective reminders of the culturally specific nature of modern Western mapping conventions. Methods for representing the physical world are myriad. The modern Mercator projection is far from necessary and natural.

Another form of mapping that bears strong resemblance to Zuni map art can be found in indigenous Mexican maps. These late sixteenth-century maps are hybrid forms reflecting both indigenous and European mapping practices, with glyphs placed on certain features of the landscape that indicate the history of ownership and use of specific sites. Thus, the physical landscape is inscribed with cultural history through a system of conventionalized visual codes.

The conventions of representation employed in Zuni map art bear striking similarities to indigenous Mexican maps. However, significant differences also exist between the two. In Zuni map art, the paintings' glyphs mark the physical sites at which such petroglyphs are found. These glyphs encode information for both the reader of the map and the reader of the cultural landscape they mark. They serve as reminders of the significance of the sites they inscribe, sites that play significant roles in larger cultural narratives.

Cultural mapping of the landscape through art has been employed as an educational tool and community-building strategy at the A:shiwi A:wan Museum and Heritage Center for some time. Upon entering the museum, the visitor encounters a floor-to-ceiling mural representing the history of the Zuni people painted by Zuni Map Art artist Ronnie Cachini, with the assistance of Zuni High School students. Starting with the Zuni Emergence near Ribbon Falls in the Grand Canyon and proceeding simultaneously through inextricably interlinked physical and traditional cultural landscapes, the cultural and the physical are collapsed into one.

Finding the museum's introductory mural an effective means of conveying community history and reinforcing Zuni identity through identification of significant connections with the surrounding land, Enote decided to expand the project. He commissioned three Zuni artists to produce easel paintings representing sites in and around the village of Zuni, and the paintings were then photographed, printed as posters, and then distributed to every Zuni household. Artists chosen for this initial phase of the project in 2006, which focused on lands the Zuni presently occupy, were Ronnie Cachini (also the primary artist of the museum's mural), who represented the Zuni reservation; Geddy Epaloose, who painted Zuni Middle Village; and Edward Wemytewa, who produced a painting representing the wider Zuni region.

Seeking to further extend the project, Enote then secured funding from private philanthropic organizations, including the Annenberg Foundation, the Christensen Fund, and the Lannan Foundation, to enable artists, in the company of religious leaders such as Octavius Seowtewa, to visit sites significant to Zuni cultural history and to commission additional paintings documenting those sites.

In this second phase of the project, artists and consultants moved beyond the confines of existing Zuni lands to sites and waterways that played important roles in ancestral Zuni lives through migration, settlement, and pilgrimage. These included the Four Corners, the Rio Grande Pueblos, Bandelier National Monument, Navajo National Monument, Grand Canyon, Chaco Canyon, and Mesa Verde; migration of one group of early Zuni ancestors southward into Mexico; and vital waterways and water sources, including the Colorado River, Little Colorado River, Zuni River, wells and springs in and around Zuni, and Zuni Salt Lake.

Over half the artists participating in the Zuni Map Art project are under the age of thirty, and their prior exposure to traditional Zuni cultural history has varied. Some were raised in traditional families that included religious leaders who have passed important knowledge on to them. Others were raised in families with little or no religious ties; thus they have acquired significant new traditional knowledge from map art project consultants. Project leaders and participants hope Zuni Map Art will serve as a model for future activity and that the younger artists who have participated will continue to produce work informed by an enhanced understanding of Zuni cultural landscapes and traditional cultural knowledge.

A striking consistency can be found in the images comprising Zuni Map Art. Nearly every work includes rock art-derived imagery. Over past centuries, sites important to Ancestral Puebloan and Zuni history and origins have been marked with petroglyphs and pictographs that serve, in rock art scholar Mary Jane Young's words, as "metonyms of narrative," wherein fragments of a larger cultural narrative serve as stand-ins or reminders of their larger context of meaning.[16] These sites are associated with meanings and memories crucial to individual and cultural identity, and the individual is bound to the group through shared understanding of their significance. Petroglyphs and pictographs function in much the same manner as Leslie Marmon Silko explains that traditional Pueblo storytelling operates. Their meaning passed on orally from one person to another, they provide present and future generations with aids for successful negotiation of the world. Through these markings, the landscape is encoded with cultural significance; and, through recording of these glyphs and the sites they mark, the maps/paintings created by these artists serve as guides to other Zunis in navigating their way through a landscape flush with signifiers of cultural history and shared identity.[17]

Jennifer McLerran is Assistant Professor of Art History at Northern Arizona University. She co-edited this catalog with Jim Enote, conducted the Zuni map artist interviews, and served as a curatorial consultant for the exhibition A:shiwi A:wan Ulohnanne - The Zuni World.

1 Leslie Marmon Silko, "Landscape, History, and the Pueblo Imagination," *Antaeus*, vol. 57 (Summer 1986): 83.
2 Author interview with Octavius Seowtewa, A:shiwi A:wan Museum and Heritage Center, Zuni, New Mexico, November 6, 2010.
3 See J. J. Brody, *Anasazi and Pueblo Painting* (Albuquerque: University of New Mexico Press, 1991) and Clara Lee Tanner, *Southwest Indian Painting* (Tucson: University of Arizona Press, 1957) and *Southwest Indian Painting: A Changing Art* (Tucson: University of Arizona Press, 1973).
4 See Bruce Bernstein and W. Jackson Rushing, *Modern By Tradition: American Indian Painting in the Studio Style* (Santa Fe: Museum of New Mexico Press, 1995); J. J. Brody, *Indian Painters and White Patrons* (Albuquerque: University of New Mexico Press, 1971) and *Pueblo Indian Painting: Tradition and Modernism in New Mexico, 1900-1930* (Santa Fe, NM: School of American Research Press and Seattle: University of Washington Press, 1997); Dorothy Dunn, *American Indian Painting of the Southwest and Plains Areas* (Albuquerque: University of New Mexico Press, 1968); and Clara Lee Tanner, *Southwest Indian Painting* (Tucson: University of Arizona Press, 1957) and *Southwest Indian Painting: A Changing Art* (Tucson: University of Arizona Press, 1973).
5 Sources on Percy Tsisete Sandy include: Clara Lee Tanner, *Southwest Indian Painting* (Tucson: University of Arizona Press, 1957), 44, 109-110; and Dorothy Dunn, *American Indian Painting of the Southwest and Plains Areas* (Albuquerque: University of New Mexico Press, 1968), 347.
6 For example, it is forbidden for Zuni women to paint or otherwise represent kachinas.
7 Sources on Anthony Edaakie include: Dorothy Dunn, *American Indian Painting of the Southwest and Plains Areas* (Albuquerque: University of New Mexico Press, 1968), 348. Sources on Theodore Edaakie include: Dorothy Dunn, *American Indian Painting of the Southwest and Plains Areas* (Albuquerque: University of New Mexico Press, 1968), 347; and J. J. Brody, *Indian Painters and White Patrons* (Albuquerque: University of New Mexico Press, 1971), 114.
8 According to Anthony Edaakie's grandson, Keith Edaakie, Anthony's brother also helped with the painting of the murals (Author interview with Keith Edaakie, A:shiwi A:wan Museum and Heritage Center, Zuni, New Mexico, October 9, 2010). I am indebted to former Pueblo Indian Cultural Center Museum Director Elizabeth Akiya Chestnut and Anthony Edaakie's wife, Rita Edaakie, for information on the De Anza Motor Lodge murals (Elizabeth Akiya Chestnut, personal communication with author, November 22, 24, 26, 2010). Chestnut, who conducted extensive interviews with Rita Edaakie at the Zuni Senior Center in October of 2010 in her capacity as Route 66 De Anza Association Project Coordinator, reports that Anthony Edaakie worked on the murals over a period of three to four years in the late 1950s, probably executing the work in casein. She further explains: "The mural on the north wall is of the Shalako participants, a Kiva leader, the Fire God, two horned dancers, the Shalako and his helper, and two mud heads. The mural on the East wall is of the Salamopias, society kiva leaders, resplendent in beautiful, inlay-like kilts, headdresses and other paraphernalia. They are led by a kiva member who is blessing the procession with corn meal." Chestnut also reports that she was "told (at another time by another Zuni individual) that Tony had 'fixed' the images so that they could be viewed without problems by non-Pueblo people."
9 Author interview with Alex Seowtewa, A:shiw A:wan Museum and Heritage Center, Zuni, New Mexico, November 6, 2010. Sources on Patone Chuyati include: Clara Lee Tanner, *Southwest Indian Painting* (Tucson: University of Arizona Press, 1957), 40, 108-109; and Dorothy Dunn, *American Indian Painting of the Southwest and Plains Areas* (Albuquerque: University of New Mexico Press, 1968), 192, 215.
10 Author interview with Alex Seowtewa, A:shiwi A:wan Museum and Heritage Center, Zuni, New Mexico, November 6, 2010.
11 Sources on ecomuseums include: Peter Davis, *Ecomuseums: A Sense of Place* (London: Leicester University Press, 1999); Nancy J. Fuller, "The Museum as a Vehicle for Community Empowerment: The Ak Chin Community Ecomuseum Project," in *Museums and Communities: The Politics of Public Culture*, edited by Ivan Karp, et al. (Washington, D.C.: Smithsonian Institution Press, 1992), 327-66; Gwyneira Isaac, *Mediating Knowledges: Origins of a Zuni Tribal Museum* (Tucson: University of Arizona Press), foreword by Jim Enote; Dominique Poulot, "Identity as Self-Discovery: The Ecomuseum in France," in *Museum Culture: Histories, Discourses, Spectacles*, edited by Daniel J. Sherman and Irit Rogoff (Minneapolis: University of Minnesota Press, 1994), 66-84; and George Henri Riviere, "The Ecomuseum—An Evolutive Definition," *Museum*, vol. 37, no. 4 (1985): 182-183; Isaac book on A:shiwi A:wan Museum and Heritage Center.
12 James Enote, Christensen Fund Application, 2010.
13 Peter Whitridge, "Landscapes, Houses, Bodies, Things: 'Place' and the Archaeology of Inuit Imaginaries," *Journal of Archaeological Method and Theory*, vol. 11, no. 2 (June 2004): 220-221.
14 As Whitridge asserts, places are significant "as the sites of attachment of the real to a space of circulation of socially intelligible significations, in which entities that are incommensurate with respect to their materialities—landscapes, houses, bodies, things—freely exchange properties in the form of conceptual attributes and symbolic associations" (Whitridge, p.20.) This representational space is the "imaginary." And as Benedict Anderson, author of *Imagined Communities*, has so cogently argued, the cultural imaginary—which is predicated on a shared understanding of culturally and historically specific signifying systems—works to construct community and place-based identity. See Benedict R. Anderson, *Imagined Communities: Reflections on the Origin and Spread of Nationalism* (London: Verso, 1991).
15 Keith H. Basso, *Wisdom Sits In Places: Landscape and Language Among the Western Apache* (Albuquerque: University of New Mexico Press, 1996).
16 M. Jane Young uses the term "metonyms of narrative" to describe the way in which rock art of the American Southwest functions metonymically, recalling whole cultural narratives and histories via single, associated images. See M. Jane Young, "Images of Power and the Power of Images: The Significance of Rock Art for Contemporary Zunis," *Journal of American Folklore*, vol. 98, no. 387 (1985): 15.
17 Much as Whitridge describes the process that occurs in Inuit mapping, in Zuni map art place in general and Zuni ancestral lands in particular become "a nexus of imaginary significations at the site of its intersection with the real" (Whitridge, p. 241).

A:shiwi A:wan Ulohnanne • The Zuni World

Emergence at Ribbon Falls, Grand Canyon; Zuni Emergence and Migration Mural at the A:shiwi A:wan Museum and Heritage Center. Photograph by Jim Enote.

Cultural Advisor Statement
Octavius Seowtewa

I started working with the [A:shiwi A:wan] museum when they first started the map art [project] a couple of years back. Working through the Zuni Cultural Preservation as a ZCRAT member got me involved with a lot of these places, but it was just information that was stored in archives and not used for the betterment of the Zuni people; and so, when I was introduced to this concept of making map art, I thought this was the avenue that I was looking for to get that information out.

   Just going to some of these places that I've known about, giving information to the staff and the artists . . . opened up a new interest of building from that and including some of the other sites that are not—were not—mentioned or not even talked about . . . like Navajo National Monument, Canyon de Chelly—you know, those were sort of off limits because . . . they're part of the Navajo tribe, Navajo Nation homelands. But, after I did some consultation work with the Navajo National Monument, I brought that information back to Jim [Enote]; and, after he looked at the sites that were there, we decided to make . . . a trip to see what was actually out there. And that first trip was overwhelming. To see one of the sites—Betatakin, especially that first one that we went to—was so identical to Mesa Verde, Canyon de Chelly and all the others that . . . we could use that information to educate our own people because they've heard about these places; but, because information wasn't readily available to the tribe or the tribal members, it was something that was just put on the back burners or just mentioned a few times. So, working . . . just with the Historic Preservation Office opened up my eyes on what we need to do.

   . . . I think we're now in the process of getting that information out in a way that—instead of putting it in books, because there's a lot of information out in books—but have people to grasp and look at the sites without actually being there. And then the interpretation from the artists themselves was so overwhelming that some of the things that are not mentioned were picked up by the artists. And, so, when we did have meetings, they'd bring their paintings in and—because I've made numerous visits to the sites, I had a little information, that, generally, "You left this out" or, you know, "Can you change this?" And, with this open dialogue with the artists, we didn't have any problems of getting the whole information out . . . through the map.

[T]he art themselves, they're beautiful, but they have a purpose now. They have a deeper meaning, because our oral history is very complex. And, because it's passed on from generation to generation. . . .

[N]ow that we've got the open door with the Park Service . . . we can go into areas that the public aren't allowed to go. So, when we got that opportunity, we try and maximize on that information. And . . . it snowballed into all this perfect information . . . that we wanted for our grandchildren. And I think that was the main thought—why I wanted to get involved with the map art [project] . . . our people here . . . now that they're so involved with computers and electronics, that that information is disappearing. So, with this type of information that we have, we're opening a whole new door for our kids and their grandkids . . . we're now connecting some of the dots to our oral history with these places.

[T]hey're grasping not only the written information, but now . . . they have a chance to look at places where they've just heard or read about . . . we can have them look at it, we can tell them where it's at. It's hard for people to . . . grasp the vastness of the [Grand] [C]anyon. But I think Ronnie [Cachini's work] is a good example of . . . all the different sites and even the quartz mine, the Supai Man. Things like that . . . were never mentioned to the Zunis, but now we have that information. We've always known about the hematite mine. There's been documented information about people going there to collect the red hematite—red ochre. And things like that that were collected in the canyon, but quartz and even the salt was never mentioned to us; but now, going through all these trips, I've made fourteen trips within the canyon, so every time I make a trip I'm gathering new information that can be used for the map art. And, so, when we did take the artists down [the river] I could see in their eyes that, you know, in fact, they did mention that they were given that information. They were told when they were growing up about what was there in that Grand Canyon, especially where we emerged from, and now they had the chance to actually be there. And just looking at their eyes and . . . just trying to get in their minds what they were thinking, but it took a while for them to start talking about it . . . they just wanted to take everything in.

[W]e never had books about where our ancestors traveled, but they left the marks there . . . for future generations to tie themselves back into these same sites that our ancestors used. And it's like a book or information that they left behind to tell us that "Yes, we were here, and your people are part of this area." And, if we can identify or interpret . . . the petroglyphs, pictographs, then it just . . . makes our oral history, our migration history, that much more . . . solid.

It gives it . . . more depth because we have this information that was left behind, and we're . . . utilizing all of that information in the map art [project].

[And] now that we have this understanding within the parks, they're getting to understand that we do need to look at those areas and maybe give our own insight or give them the information about what that paint is, or how it was put on there, because they weren't using paint brushes and they used to use mitts made out of rabbit skin to put the whitewash and the paints on it. So, with that type of information, the Park Service [is] getting valuable information from us. But, then, we're also getting good information back, so I think it's getting to be a good working relationship with all the parks. And, now that [they] are finding out what we're doing or what type of information we're giving out, their open door policy is helping both the Park Service and us.

I've had two grandfathers that had a lot of information and I still go back to some of their words when I talk about things or trying to give the right information to whoever wants to . . . know about Zuni or understand Zuni. Because of them, I've got so much information . . . with their help and their wisdom . . . I look at things and I think about it and . . . tie things together, and look and say "I think this is what it's saying."

[Zuni Map Art is] historical. It's very important that we're doing this, not only for the museum but for the Zuni people and for the rest of the world because we have artifacts that are out there in England, Japan, Canada, Switzerland . . . and some of the artifacts are incorporated in the paintings. So, you know, it gives us more leverage to deal with the museums now that we have this information.

I'm glad we have Jim that had the foresight to do something like this. I've always wanted a different avenue to get that information out, not only to the people that are going to the parks but our own people, too, because as I mentioned that some of them don't have the opportunity to make a trip down the canyon; and, when I came back there was a lot of people that grilled me for information, and now we have the paintings. And I can turn around and say, "Remember I was telling you about this? Remember I found this there?" And, so, it's there now and . . . we have these artists that are gifted that . . . have their own way of painting.

Cultural Advisor Statement
Curtis Quam

The map art paintings . . . are educational tools . . . for our community people and also for outsiders to see through Zuni eyes . . . . Within the Zuni language, the English language, the translation of both of those sometimes gets lost within translation. But within a visual form, it's right there, it's right in front of you.

[W]ithin the village . . . it really kind of helps also promote art and promote how powerful art is to a lot of kids here. And I think it really . . . opens a lot of their eyes and their imagination into a lot of the places that are important to us . . . and how they can convey that . . . . Knowing what's sensitive, knowing what's not, and what's appropriate . . . they can convey their culture through different types of art forms . . . . But beyond the village, I think it really shows the Zuni's presence in a lot of these areas. I know before we started this whole painting series, the Zuni presence was . . . barely mentioned . . . . Now, with paintings like these, outside people can see how important these places are and what the relationships are to Zuni. . . .

. . . [T]he museum helped a lot because we provided a lot of outreach on all these paintings through different schools and different sites to make people aware that these places are important, especially for our community. I think that's where it really helps—that we had a museum here to get all that information out so people know that these places are important. . . . People would never have a chance to see places like the Grand Canyon or Mesa Verde, Chaco Canyon, Navajo National Monument. They can actually see those areas if they come to the museum or if they come in and see all the trips that we've taken and see all our photos—not just the paintings but the photos that we have—the resource that the school, the community and non-community members can use as a resource.

. . . [E]very meeting, every trip, every discussion that we had, we always came out of it with something new. I grew up knowing . . . some of what was . . . being discussed. . . . But specific places were very new to me. Our emergence and migration history, I kind of grew up with a lot of that teaching within my family. . . . So I kind of already had that background and that interest, but just taking site visits to these areas, it was something very new.

[For the artists] . . . Ronnie [Cachini, for example] . . . I just wanted to get him more of the Colorado Rivers, the headwaters of the Colorado Rivers, the tributaries and all the way to the ocean. Getting those maps and getting the different angles, different pictures through books, through on-line research . . . so I did a lot of that research. . . . [W]e took a lot of pictures and . . . made copies for the artists so they could use them in their painting. . . . One of the biggest highlights for me was doing the research.

We wanted to get to areas that were as intact and undisturbed as possible . . . like Inscription House, which is closed off to [most] visitors, and we made that hike and it was a very long and very hot hike. . . . We also had different cultural advisement, like Octavius . . . would tell us what came from that area. And one of the more interesting things I heard at Inscription House was . . . feathers [were found] that were in the order that we use here, and also reeds that were used in cigarettes . . . that made it very significant, because that's what we use here today in a lot of our ceremonial offerings. . . . Each place had something like that, either . . . an artifact or a spring . . . where our ancestors used to collect water, drink water. And these sites that we visited we know . . . the ancestors of our people still occupy those areas.

. . . Working with students and . . . doing a lot of the cultural education here at the museum . . . I can actually say "Yeah, I've been to this area. . . ." It weighs more with the kids when you can actually say "I've been here. I've done this. I've experienced how difficult it was." Or "I felt that presence of our ancestors in these areas. . . ." And we can kind of relay that to our community members, not just kids . . . and say "This is why it's important to us" and "This is what I felt. This is what I experienced then" and "This is what we did when we were there."

. . . I've noticed that every presentation that I've done in the classrooms or anywhere else . . . some of the photos that we have from all our trips and the experiences that we have really brought the presentation to life. And it's kind of hard to imagine having teen-age kids all be quiet during class, during presentations, but so far that's the reaction that we've got during presentations that we've done.

A:shiwi A:wan Ulohnanne • The Zuni World

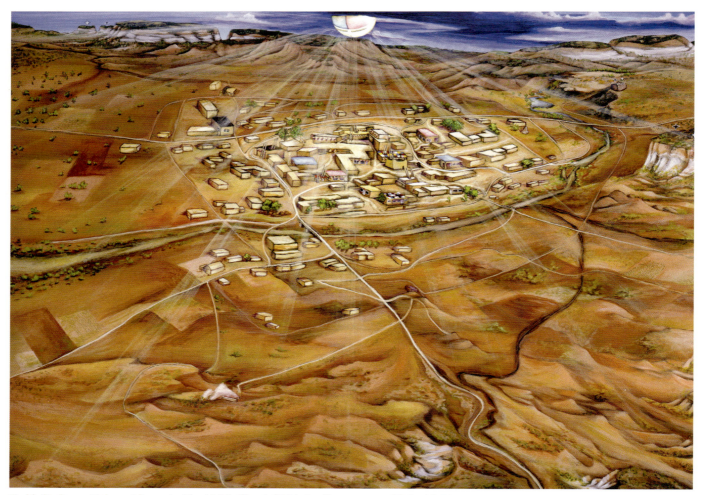

Geddy Epaloose, Halona: Idiwana'a (The Middle Place), 2006. Acrylic on canvas, 33.5 x 43.5 in.

Artist Statement
Geddy Epaloose

I think at this time in the world everything is so fast, people are moving so fast, days come by and go so that we tend to forget our roots and what really makes us. And so I think we see other people, tribes, going one direction, sort of trying to look out for financial interests, and we are kind of stuck trying to hold onto one part of our lives and yet trying to keep up with the rest of the world, and that's like a struggle, but then that is what makes us. So I think it's important that this project came about because it really gives the younger generation an idea of history and different sites that were used in history.

We hear these site names and place names in prayers, songs, and repeatedly, but you can only visualize in your head what it actually looks like and maybe you might not—you probably shouldn't for your own safety—visualize some of them, but you can't help but to. And this is like a tool to bridge that gap—oral history and visual history. So, I think we're doing a pretty good thing, doing justice in that way.

My paintings, in particular, I try to take significant elements, objects and incorporate them into my paintings. And these objects are most basic but yet most important. For example, one object is the sun, and that's how it all began, this whole history and up to the present day . . . a basic element, the sun, but so important at the same time. Without his calling, the people wouldn't be where they are today . . . they call it the Zia symbol, but it's not. It's the sun—the Father Sun.

You learn from other artists around you. The artists I'm currently involved with in this project are artists that I actually looked up to when I was still younger than teenage years. I looked up to the artists that are involved in this project, and that's inspiration in itself to even . . . have your name mentioned amongst this circle of artists.

The focal point on the [Grand Canyon] painting is . . . Ribbon Falls and the other sites that outlie it. . . . So you have Ribbon Falls in the middle. Above it is Upper Ribbon Falls, where actually they migrated from when they came up. And they built just above. So that's depicted, along with basic designs, sort of a map of how the Grand Canyon, the Colorado River, is in relation geographically to Zuni. Just to give the audience an idea that there is still that relationship there, and it's not that far if you think about it.

Geddy Epaloose, K'ya'na: K'yawakwayina A:dehya (Ojo Caliente), 2009. Acrylic on canvas, 40 x 30 in.

Geddy Epaloose, Chimik'yana'kya dey'a (Ribbon Falls), 2010. Acrylic on canvas, 48 x 36 in.

[Referring to another painting] I titled that Kya'na, which is that spring right on the top right corner, and that is named Kya'na. So that and the sites around it is how you would—how I would interpret it in English. . . . It's a spring, and there's several other springs outlying that spring. . . . [And] the deer are significant to that site because it is another form of Shalako. . . . As research and study, I usually use photographs just to get the scale, light. Sometimes I just do it on my own, I don't study, but on that painting I did. The [photos] come from the archives here. This is always the place to go when you need research. . . . .

Ronnie Cachini really helped me get over the second half of that painting . . . as an artist, he's a good advisor. And it's kind of good to get advice from an artist because you know they're talking from a perspective of an artist. . . . probably without him helping me, it wouldn't have come out. It would have come out different. . . . He gave me a lot of insight in the area, stories, background, what things meant, and that really finished the painting.

[On one trip it]. . . really helped because Octavius [Seowtewa] and Curtis [Quam] both accompanied me. [And another trip] we did . . . a flyover . . . that was cool.

[For the Grand Canyon trip] there's no words to explain that. It was cool . . . . It was something that I . . . could only dream of. . . . Of course, you could only imagine what it would be like and think and try to get that feeling, but nothing as close as actually seeing it and feeling what it felt like. It was very moving to visit some of these sites.

. . . My [influences were] teachers here, family members, uncles that used to paint in high school, just looking at their work, painting, watercolors. Different teachers I had in middle school in Zuni and also high school in Flagstaff. . . .

Well, I hope it [Zuni Map Art] helps people . . . know that this area was first inhabited by the Zuni people and should not be claimed by other peoples as their own. . . . And I also hope that the audience, when they see these paintings, get an idea of [how] we're really rich in our beliefs and our culture, history, and we really can back it up. We're showing you that it's not a story. It's history. . . ."

I want my audience to feel my paintings . . . it's going to be different for a Zuni to visualize, or see my painting and take in that information. It might mean more to them than it does to anyone else, but I'm okay with that. That's what this project is for . . . down the line you're gonna know that you were involved in a great project—this one. . . . We are probably the first to do this, so people can only copy.

Artist Statement
Ronnie Cachini

The reservation map [artwork] was pretty simple. Living and growing up here all my life, I basically know the reservation like the back of my hand. So that wasn't . . . too much of a problem, but the Colorado River was quite a challenge. I had to do research on it, where the river started . . . and how [it] meandered . . . . Our ancestors used this river to go to the Sea of Cortez and to the Pacific Ocean where they collected shells and salt water. . . . They used the Colorado River to travel to and from.

And when our ancestors went out on these pilgrimages, they would go out for years. It took them three, four years before they would come back. And, along the way, they would settle, make their houses. So there's settlements all along the corridor of the Colorado River, all the way to the Sea of Cortez, and there's potsherds that were found that are similar to our ancestors'. So, and from our great-great-grandfathers talking about our people traveling [to] the Pacific Ocean . . . we know that they used the rivers as roadways to get to places. So rivers are very important to our people. . . .

[O]ur reservation has hundreds of ancestral sites, but we don't believe in exposing them . . . because the spirits are still there. . . . Our . . . Zuni Cultural Advisory Team . . . we go and view different sites . . . and we're trying to let the Park Service know that our ancestral homeland was quite vast. . . . Our ancestors emerged from the fourth underworld in the Grand Canyon, where we know as Ribbon Falls. And, from there, they had come up from the Grand Canyon and started settling along the Sunset Crater and . . . Canyon Diablo. And they were told to search for the Middle Place. And, at Diablo Canyon, they had split into three parties. The medicine societies . . . they went up north . . . . And our people, they followed the Little Colorado to the Zuni Heavens. And then, the third party, they went down south, which we've never seen again. And the medicine societies . . . settled in various places, like Chaco Canyon, Mesa Verde, Navajo Monument, Aztec, just along there. And they were told to settle for four days, which we know is not four days, but four years, four hundred years, or forty years. So they had settled and stayed there for quite a while and then traveled on. . . . They used the stars. They used the sun, the moon . . . as a calendar.

And we know this because the medicine societies, they sing about the stars, the universe, and basically the creation of the world. . . . [T]hen they traveled here to Zuni, to Petroglyph Monument, to Mount Taylor, El Morro, to Nutria, and the Kivas of the Great Ruins, and then finally meeting up with our people here in Zuni. So those medicine mans are the ones who brought that knowledge here, through traveling up north. . . .

This was a very highly spiritual world which they lived in . . . it's these events that happened . . . that we recite in our prayers. . . . The connection with us, the Zuni people, through the Grand Canyon, is a invisible umbilical cord. We still have ties, we have our prayers that tells us about where our people had originated from. And we have prayers about how everything was created, how we as Zuni people were created by the two twin War Gods. . . . It's this knowledge that's been handed down from generation to generation that keeps us going. . . .

And . . . these . . . maps, we are able to . . . teach our young children—our people—that Zuni, here, Holona: Idiwana'a isn't the only place that we've known, that we have a spiritual tie to. . . . you can go out for a whole week and not visit all of them . . . just in the vicinity of the village, in the inner village, outer village, and then the mesas, and then outside the reservation, all over. . . . [S]o we still have these ties to these places—Mt. Taylor, and there's San Francisco Peak. These places are considered as medicine. They're highly regarded to the medicine societies. These medicine societies are the keepers . . . of knowledge, in how to cure and maintain life . . . . There are sensitivities to these areas because of [the] highly spiritual beings there . . . springs and just any kind of waterways, it's a spirit, it's a living entity. That's the flesh of our ancestors. Water, raindrops are the flesh of our ancestors. So, when it rains, we say our grandfathers are coming . . . .

I hope that the map art will continue to help our people, especially the young children, so that they won't forget who they are and where they came from, and how our ancestors lived, and where they had traveled. And it's not just the vicinity of Zuni . . . . It's clear up to Utah and southern Colorado, most of New Mexico and Arizona. . . .

[On the Colorado River] there are rock outcrops there that have petroglyphs all over. . . . There's two of them that have nothing but continuous lines—squares, straight lines. . . . Some have stars, some have spirals. And it's a map. It's a map of the river . . . . When I saw that rock . . . it just . . . stuck in my head. I just kept visualizing that rock. And so, I said, "I'm gonna make them a rock." So my whole painting is of that rock. And there's sites incorporated along the way from Lee's Ferry all the way down to Diamond Creek.

Ronnie Cachini

Ronnie Cachini, Ho'n A:wan Dehwa:we (Our Land), 2006. Acrylic on canvas, 33.5 x 43.5 in.

A:shiwi A:wan Ulohnanne • The Zuni World

Ronnie Cachini, Sites in the Grand Canyon, 2010. Acrylic on canvas, 30 x 40 in.

Ronnie Cachini, Colorado River, 2009. Acrylic on canvas, 33 x 43 in.

A:shiwi A:wan Ulohnanne • The Zuni World

Edward Wemytewa, K'yawakwayina:we (Waterways), 2006. Oil on canvas, 36 x 48 in.

Artist Biography
Edward Wemytewa

Edward Wemytewa is a playwright, performer, and visual artist whose paintings and sculpture have been shown in museums in Arizona and New Mexico. He is a founding director of Idiwanan An Chawe, a storytelling theater, and served as a Zuni Tribal Councilman. His painting, K'yawakwayina:we (Waterways) is one of the first Map Art works commissioned by the A:shiwi A:wan Museum and Heritage Center.

Joey Zunie, Four Corners, 2008. Acrylic on canvas, 42 x 33 in.

Artist Statement
Joey Zunie

I got selected for the Four Corners area, and so—the painting it involves just mainly our ancestors' sites . . . Mesa Verde and Canyon de Chelly and even Chaco Canyon, and it has Zuni here and some places up in Utah and just surrounding landmarks that you . . . could distinguish as a map to see. And the colors there involve the directions, the north, east, south, and west, using our religious colors. They were given to those directions. And the . . . sun face there is our Sun Father, and he is very important to our religion and . . . what we . . . pray to . . . he's our god and without him we wouldn't have life. It's just people, crops, animals, you know. So I involved him because I think he's very important to our culture and religion. . . . [T]he petroglyphs are from the areas that are involved . . . and so there's corn plants on there. Corn is very important, too . . . it's sustained us with life and we still farm today and everywhere those places are on the painting there is . . . evidence of farming and so corn is our life here, too.

I think it's a very important project for the younger generation to use as a learning tool . . . some of the young generation they're not really involved in religion now or they might not be hearing the stories that we have heard . . . they can hear stories and they can visually see what the places are and where they're at. So I think that's a very good opportunity. . . .

I was fortunate when I was younger to hear many of the oral stories . . . that were told by some of the elders that have passed on and . . . just to listen to them and try to put together everything imagined in your head. . . . What the scene is and what's happening. . . .

[In the Grand Canyon painting] I have four sites that I'm doing . . . one of Lava Falls Cave . . . it's mainly about pictographs on a nice, good-sized boulder. The other one will be a hematite mine . . . where the Zunis collect red paint that we use. And the more famous one will be the Whitmore Wash—paintings on the rock wall . . . that tells of our origin and creation—how we came from the underworlds. It's visually there on the rock, and it's very meaningful . . . just to actually see . . . what our oral story. . . is right there in the Grand Canyon on the wall painted. . . . The last place will be Three Springs. This is another place that has paintings on the rock walls, and there's some grinding stones.

A:shiwi A:wan Ulohnanne · The Zuni World

Joey Zunie, Lava Falls, Opposite Three Springs, and Hematite Mine, 2010. Acrylic on canvas, 36 x 48 in.

Joey Zunie

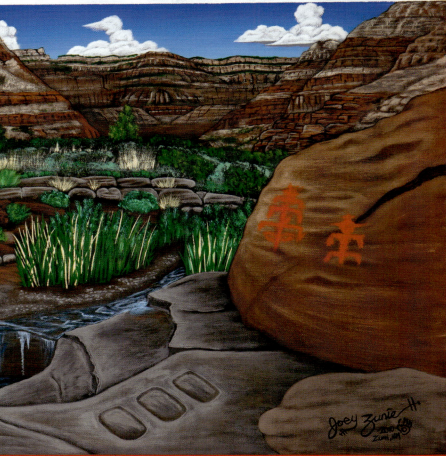

Joey Zunie, Chaco Canyon, 2011. Acrylic on canvas, 36 x 48 in.

The [Grand Canyon] trip was wonderful. It was just a life experience to . . . travel with other members of the community—advisors, artists—to go down there as a group to see all the places that will be on the paintings. It was a life experience just to go down there for fourteen days and river rafting and seeing our religious places, and it was fun. I'll never forget it. [Octavius Seowtewa] would tell us . . . what the place meant and what was there, and from there I usually would ask him questions . . . just to get a better understanding of what the sites were and what they mean . . . he was there every day. He was our teacher. Usually during the nighttime we'd gather around and have our talks and just discussion of the day's activities . . . getting each others' input and advice and what could be done with these paintings.

[The Chaco Canyon painting is] mainly about the Chaco Culture and how Zuni's very related to that place, and I think that's one place . . . that needs to be documented with the map art project, just to tie in with all these other places that are happening with the paintings. . . . We actually got the royal treatment out there with the Park Service. It was very nice, and they worked with us very well. . . . [Sites in the painting are] mainly in the Chaco area. And maybe probably some surrounding areas on the outskirts of the Chaco region . . . lots of petroglyphs I'll put in there.

I'm home alone and I paint, so, while the family's out working or at school . . . I have one daughter . . . she just turned twelve . . . she's actually trying to take over my easel . . . she's already messing with my paints.

When I'm not painting, I do the fetish carvings, and I also do mascot and lettering work on gym floors—basketball gym floors. Yeah, I've done several schools. I've put their logo on and do the lettering so they have a nice basketball court to play on. Then, yeah, I mean, it's art, any kind of art, that I do.

[Artist] Phil Hughte, who's passed on . . . he did real nice work . . . mainly his colors and the way he uses colors and his cartoon work, too. It's probably those guys, you know, that I kind of looked up to them in wanting to be what they accomplished through their art . . . that's how I looked at myself.

A:shiwi A:wan Ulohnanne • The Zuni World

Duane Dishta, Grand Canyon, 2009. Acrylic on canvas, 49 x 37 in.

Artist Biography
Duane Dishta

Duane Dishta illustrated Barton Wright's book *Kachinas of the Zuni*, and his work is featured in *Zuni: The Art and the People*, Vol 2. With the popularity of Native American jewelry during the 1970s, Duane briefly created silver and turquoise jewelry but returned to painting full time in the 1980s. He has created two paintings for the Map Art collection including Grand Canyon and Journey of Zuni Ancestors to the Land of Everlasting Summer.

A:shiwi A:wan Ulohnanne • The Zuni World

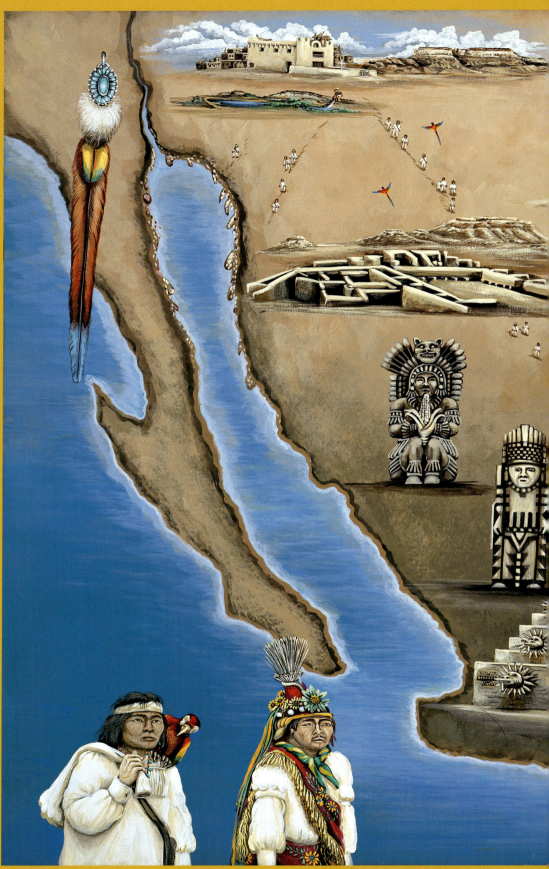

Duane Dishta, Journey of the Zuni Ancestors to the Land of Everlasting Summer, 2008.
Acrylic on canvas, 36 x 48 in.

Duane Dishta

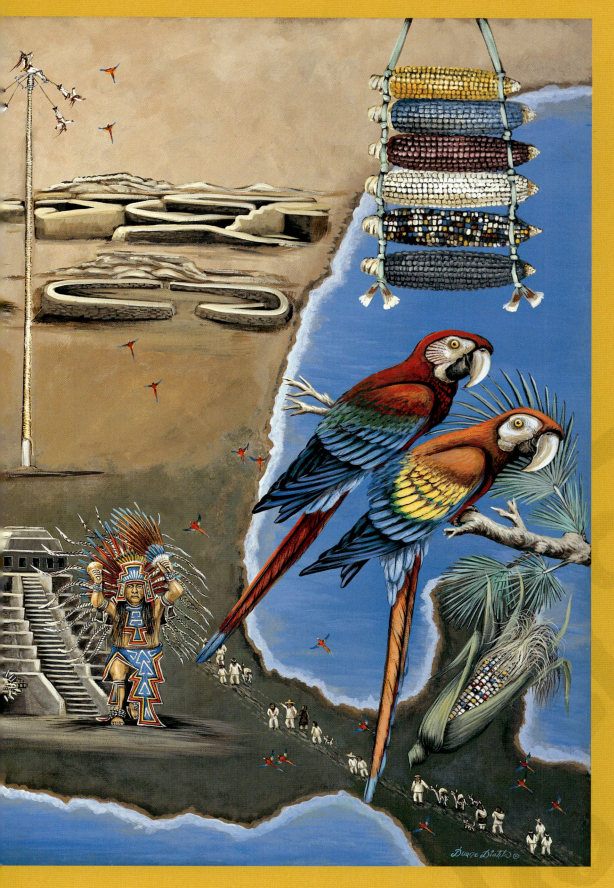

Levon Loncassion, Shiba:bulima (Bandelier National Monument), 2008. Oil on canvas, 41 x 31 in.

Artist Statement
Levon Loncassion

The first painting that I was selected to do was Bandelier National Monument, and my first idea, or ideas, I have about the map art project was . . . like a lot of the things that I was kind of thinking about but not really quite put in a context in terms of . . . an actual working map. So it was interesting to run into Jim [Enote] at that same moment . . . where I was kind of thinking about maps and map arts, but he kind of put it all together . . . in terms of putting . . . place names and cultural-specific sites to be . . . documented and . . . share that information with the rest of the community, and I thought it was just a really cool idea. . . .

[T]he second painting that I was asked to do was on the Rio Grande Pueblos, which I think for me was a really interesting situation that I found myself trying to [compose] this map, this painting, and . . . it was . . . the most difficult painting I've ever done . . . technically and compositionally. I think each painting seems to have . . . that process in it, but for this one I think it was a little bit more of a challenge. . . . I think the second painting for me was a huge accomplishment. . . . [T]hat's . . . something that comes through a lot in the whole map art project because there's a lot of information that you want to be able to convey or to express in this limited area, you know, and at the same time kind of keep . . . everything oriented to . . . what I think is kind of like how you would read a map I guess you would say. So it was quite a challenge. . . .

It's very important . . . in terms of how it just gives us . . . Indian people [a chance] to . . . tell our side of the story and to at least kind of give our viewpoint on how we see the world and how things are not as they seem to be in certain cases in terms of like Native cultures; a lot of our identity is . . . within the land. And it's . . . important in many different ways. I think it's also important for us to start making an effort to make choices to have . . . all this information available for generations to come, and it has to start somewhere, and I think with this map art project it's definitely a big start and a lot of information that is being gathered and stored and hopefully going to be shared for years to come. And I think that's . . . a really significant part of the map art project.

A:shiwi A:wan Ulohnanne • The Zuni World

Levon Loncassion, Deer Springs and Havasu Creek, 2010. Watercolor on paper, 47 x 20 in.

Levon Loncassion

A:shiwi A:wan Ulohnanne • The Zuni World

Levon Loncassion, Tribes of the Rio Grande, 2009. Watercolor on paper, 49 x 39 in.

And . . . I think all the conversations that I've had with people . . . I tell them what I'm involved in and I tell them about the map art project, and ultimately what I keep coming back to is kind of like this strange . . . political statement that it seems to be playing. [T]hough it's not . . . blatantly obvious, I think there's those reference points where it could be . . . a significant political statement as well, like challenging whoever authority it might be like the Bureau of Land Management, the Park Service, or state or federal governments, you know. It sends a message . . . we are definitely conscious of . . . our efforts to have our presence on this land known . . . . I've talked to other Pueblo Indians from the Rio Grande area and then they are just like totally excited about what we're doing . . . what is happening here in Zuni. [On visits to the Rio Grande Pueblos] I took a road trip to Taos. I took the high road to Taos through the mountains and then soon after Jim had invited me to take a plane ride to Taos, and I think that plane ride . . . gave me a better perspective on how to approach the composition of the painting because it definitely put things together. Things you couldn't quite see when you were driving down the road, you can definitely see when you're birds-eye view flying over, and so I think that's been key.

[The Grand Canyon trip] has definitely changed . . . who I am . . . spiritually. . . an overwhelming . . . understanding of . . . all the things that I've been taught, you know, like not taught but told, like stories, mythologies, and the creation story, and to have been able to go there and see it . . . firsthand, it definitely changed something inside of me, and definitely really, really amazing opportunity to be a part of. . . . I still can't believe how fortunate I was to be a part of that.

I don't really have any immediate family members who are involved in . . . the doings that are going around here in Zuni, and so . . . to be a part of something like that, that I don't really have much of an access to just because of who my family members are like uncles and fathers and what not, not being able to be a part of that, I absorbed every little bit of the experience that I could. . . . So, yeah, definitely, I learned a lot.

[M]aking that Rio Grande Pueblos painting . . . one of the requirements was to convey the Pueblo Revolt, and so there's like these split scenes of . . . battles . . . and I kind of felt uneasy about maybe being too graphic about it . . . I don't know, it might come across a little bit more like hostile . . . but then again I guess if they know that . . . the painting is depicting the Pueblo Revolt then I think it would explain things a lot more clearly than just like the visual, figurative cues on the painting itself. . . .

Being part [of Zuni Map Art is] bringing to life . . . an idea or . . . a story and . . . giving it . . . a visual reference for people to . . . make them understand a little bit more and I've always liked that about other artists.

Mallery Quetawki, Grand Canyon, 2008. Acrylic on canvas, 34 x 44 in.

Artist Statement
Mallery Quetawki

[For Zuni Map Art] I did the Grand Canyon area . . . an area that women are not allowed to go. So my entire piece is based on pictures and . . . a sense of the Grand Canyon itself. I've seen the Grand Canyon, though. I was a lot younger, and it's just so grand you remember. So, based on that and pictures and verbal descriptions I guess you could say, helped me kind of put it together. That was the hardest part, though, not getting to go. . . . It's a very sacred site—the Ribbon Falls area, the area of our creation, our emergence from the four worlds. And places and areas like that are really held in high reverence . . . a lot of things are barred from women; but, as a Zuni woman, I respect that, and I have no problem. I know where I'm from and I know what I can or cannot do. . . .

[The map art project is] really a way for us as Zunis to help document a lot of our oral traditions because you hear in our prayers about these places like Ribbon Falls . . . which I thought was just a word in our chants. The word Denetsali Ima was actually a place, and I had to ask my grandfather, I said "What is it?" and he said "It's a place for medicine men, the medicine societies." And so just knowing and documenting places like that through art—and art being a big staple in the Zuni community—putting the two together, it's really a great idea and. . . . I love it because it's a teaching tool more than anything, documenting and teaching for those of us who maybe don't know and those who want to know.

. . . There were things I did not know, like I said, and I learned. And it's really helped me, also, with my current projects. It was . . . a stepping ladder for my current endeavors, and it's going great, and I commend the museum for starting it up. It's . . . benefiting now, because they . . . made copies and gave them to the households of the village. And . . . you walk into a house and they have it displayed proudly, so it's great to see.

Everybody—they came together. It's like that's our whole . . . tradition right there, just that one small group [Zuni Map Art advisory team] hold a ton of valuable information for us and for the future, and it's . . . the idea of them allowing us to do this actually. Because a lot of things we can't document.

Either we can't because we're barred from due to religious taboos or it's just . . . impossible, and there's certain things that are. [And because] I'm not allowed to be in some of those areas . . . just verbally hearing what the place looks like and what significance it has, it was very helpful and it taught me a lot. Just the painting itself taught me a lot, not just the technicalities of it, but what's actually portrayed in it . . . [and] the idea of making a map but not making it look like . . . a road map. . . . I think that was not so much the goal as having it as a cultural landmark . . . symbolically located . . . more than it's about mapping it out, gridding it out into the roadside map kind of a style; so that was the hardest part, but it was really helpful for the advisors to tell you "Oh, you know, this is also here. And you know that there's this area around the corner," or they would tell you the significance. They just won't say "Oh, it looks like this," but they'll tell you what the significance is of that place, so that was really neat.

I went to school [the University of New Mexico] and took art classes, art history classes, and I got to see Matisse, Monet. For some reason, they didn't do much for me, but I'd still come back and think about "Oh, I want to be like Duane Dishta." I want to be like him, I want to be like Alex [Seowtewa], I want to have that. . . . It's a lot of respect there, and I enjoy them being around still for me to get to seek advice from, so you can learn from them.

I remember growing up—I was still real little, I think I was barely walking—I'd sit on his lap [father Arlen Quetawki, Sr.] and he'd just have like a blank paper and a pencil and he would draw something. I remember first seeing a duck. He's like "Your turn," and I would draw, I would try to copy his duck. We would do that back and forth a lot. And I never used to get in trouble for drawing on my mom's walls, which was kind of funny. I think my family molded me into an artist. . . .

I'm still on a mission that I've been working on for a while about the idea of combining traditional and contemporary art together, just probably the number one hardest thing as a Native artist because there's the thin red line between the two. One side says "Oh, it's too traditional," and one side says "It's not contemporary enough" or "It's too contemporary, it's not, it shouldn't be called Native art". . . . It's a boundary I'm trying to walk along or cross both sides and . . . a good research goal is to keep going, to expand myself, to try to get out there both to show for . . . the Zuni people that they understand my artwork and don't look at it as just like "Wow, okay… it's really artsy, but I don't get it." I don't want people to think about my art like that; and, yet again, I don't want the contemporary world to say "Oh, it's too realistic . . . It's too safe."

Artist Statement
Keith Edaakie

I've done three pieces. . . . First was the Zuni River Basin. . . . And then also of the Navajo National Monument, of the three sites they have over there, and I'm currently working on the one from the Grand Canyon trip. The site I got was Nankoweep, so right now what I am doing is the whole canyon, of what they consider Nankoweep, and then also the granaries. And mainly . . . that piece is . . . kind of looking back several thousand years ago at what they would have looked like when people still inhabited the area . . . people doing various activities and then also the structures of the place. . . .

[In the river basin painting] . . . the only time we see a river [at Zuni] is when there's rain or snow that has melted. Other than that . . . we have a dry riverbed and I'm just showing people what kind of things happened when we did have a river. . . . This is something that is still part of our culture. Like you see the farming, the agricultural part of it . . . and then the most important thing—the wildlife—you see a lot of birds on there. We do have a lot of . . . religious activities to where we do use feathers of a lot of those birds and . . . now it's kind of hard to come by. . . . [W]hen there was still a river, you know, you could just go in our back yards, there was willows all over where they would come in and they would feed and they would come around. . . . Some of . . . those birds you might catch a glimpse here and there, but it's very rare that you see them around anymore. . . .

[E]ven just basic day-to-day life . . . it's been changed to where . . . hardly any people farm because it's so hard to get the water and irrigate their farms. So I think . . . it's a good . . . documentation of . . . something that we had and this is something we still can have if we find people that want this back in our village. . . . Also it has a lot of significance to our religion and our culture with the two people in the lower corner—the gentleman making food offerings in the river and then also . . . just day- to-day basic essentials. The lady's getting the water and that's basically everything they use for cooking, watering, drinking, washing. So water was very important in our life and still is.

[The second painting is set in]. . . Navajo National Monument, and being that it's in the Navajo Reservation . . . people think . . . it's relating to Navajo people. [B]ut I think that's one thing that we wanted to get across . . . even though it's in

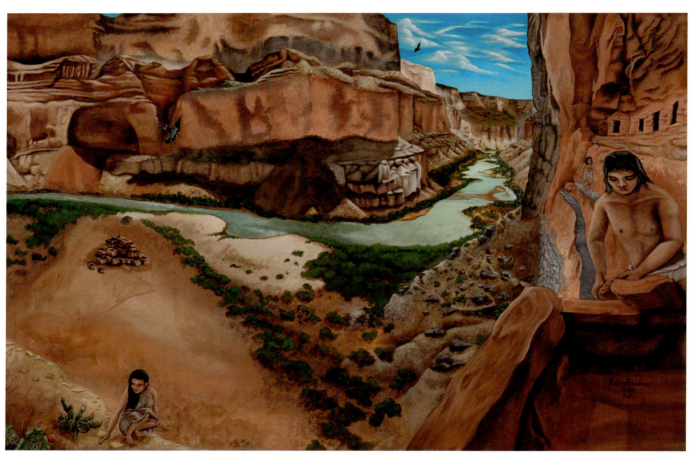

Keith Edaakie, Nankoweep, 2010. Acrylic on canvas, 36 x 54 in.

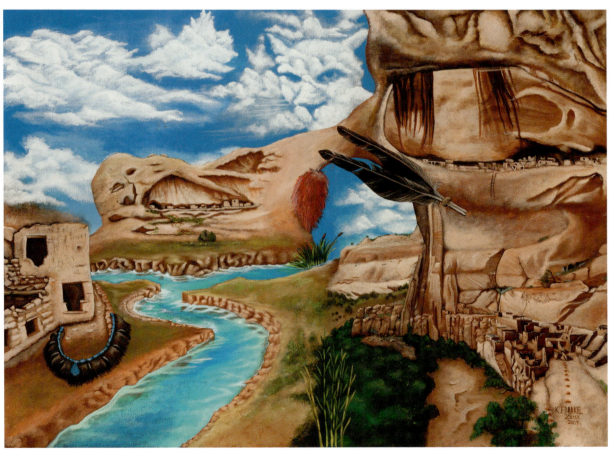

Keith Edaakie, Bishla:shiwani A:wan Heshoda:we (Navajo National Monument), 2009. Acrylic on canvas, 30 x 40 in.

A:shiwi A:wan Ulohnanne • The Zuni World

Keith Edaakie, Zuni River Basin, 2009. Acrylic on canvas, 32.5 x 42.5 in.

the Navajo Reservation there's still significance to our people, which actually it does belong to our people. Well, not just Zuni people, but, you know, what they refer to as Anasazi people. And we consider ourselves the descendants from them . . . in our migration journey there's a part . . . where the group of people separated into different ways, and we believe that's one of the sites where a couple of the medicine fraternities headed up north and made those sites there, and so there's some depictions of different things that the medicine fraternities use. . . . [T]he necklace is one thing that they use and the feathers . . . and then the red eagle plume that is hanging, too. And then also . . . there's a mountain lion depicted in the clouds, and that's one of the animals that they refer to as part of the medicine fraternities. So there was three sites there . . . two of them we visited [Betatakin and Inscription House].

[The Grand Canyon trip] . . . was one of those once-in-a-lifetime opportunities. . . . [I]t was very touching to actually see where our creation started and actually see some of the earlier sites. A lot of the sites we see are a lot older but . . . going back to where I guess you could say it all began, it was really something else. So I really did like that trip and just being away. . . .

[W]hen we want to learn something we don't put it in our brains. We put it here [gesturing to his heart], and that's where it always stays. If we put it here [gesturing to his head], over time it's going to get lost, but if you put it in your heart it's going to stay there forever. So just thinking really deeply and just really praying . . . looking for answers. It was a real good trip to take, and it was quite an experience. I've never been on a river raft before. I've never seen white water before. So, yeah, just a lot of different experiences. . . .

I always looked up [to] my Grandpa—my late Grandpa, Anthony Edaakie. He . . . and his brother Theodore Edaakie were well-known artists. . . . [A]nother person that I consider my grandpa, too, is Alex Seowtewa, . . . I think a lot of the wealth that he had he shared with me—some of the things that I do depict on my paintings . . . as an artist I really looked up to him.

[Zuni Map Art] gives us credibility . . . a lot of our information, a lot of our history, really isn't documented . . . within books or any publishing, so I think with this it gives us that documentation. . . . This is where our ancestors were, and this is where they have always been, and this is considered one of our sites when they journeyed on their migration. . . .

[Also] I think that would be good for our community as far as . . . letting them know, this is what used to happen, and this is what we have now, and this is what it looked like back then. . . . I think a lot of our people are very visual learners … when they see they understand it better, and I think with some of these we can use these as teaching aids as far as teaching our people.

A:shiwi A:wan Ulohnanne • The Zuni World

Clayton Edaakie, Great Zuni Flood, 2009. Acrylic on canvas, 33 x 43 in.

Artist Biography
Clayton Edaakie

Clayton Edaakie has two works in the A:shiwi A:wan Museum and Heritage Center's collection, including his painting of the Great Flood and the Emergence and Migration Mural, collaboratively completed by several Zuni artists. Clayton's family is very active in creating traditional Zuni fine art.

A:shiwi A:wan Ulohnanne • The Zuni World

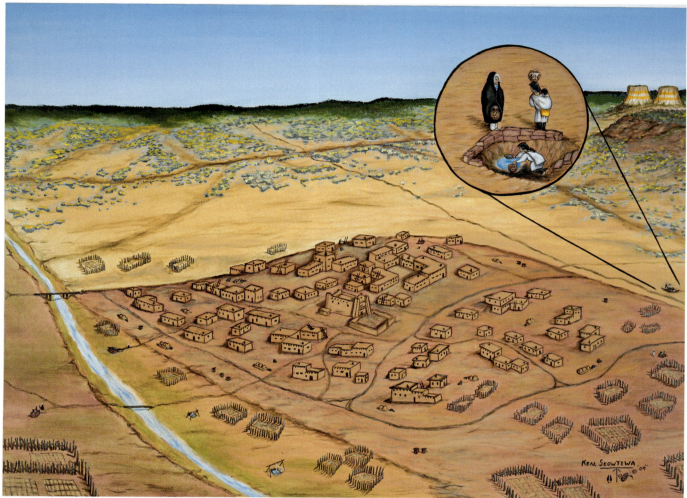

Ken Seowtewa, I Remember..., 2009. Oil on canvas, 33 x 43 in.

Artist Statement
Ken Seowtewa

Being an oral-speaking group of people, sometimes our elders, the people that hold the knowledge, pass away . . . . Through the artwork that these maps are being created . . . we've gathered information from our elders that we're trying to put down in a visual form . . . .

[P]eople in this world have their roots, their identity . . . through oral stories, through visual art, through artifacts, whatever, this is the story that other people are relating to their descendants . . . . In a sense it's a heritage that has been started . . . something that we as artists want to leave as a story to our next generations to come through.

[T]his was my first trip to the Grand Canyon. [B]ut coming . . . from a . . . family that has . . . passed the stories down . . . not just the stories, but the holy religious positions through the centuries, I've always thought stories of Grand Canyon, our Emergence . . . places that just through stories, through traditions that we've been told, but to actually witness this the first time . . . it brought tears to my eyes . . . because, knowing that . . . our history has been passed down, to actually view these sites itself was awe-inspiring to me . . . .

I was born in 1957. . . . The river . . . which is the theme of my painting, was still flowing through. . . . [A]s kids we would be swimming in there, fish there. . . . And on top of this, I still remember my grandmother was born in the late 1800s, she even asked me one time as a young boy if I could help make her kya'kwe'we, which is "houses" in our language. And in my young mind I thought we were gonna build sand castles. It was just along the river where . . . we went down and she started to make walls to a certain degree. She walked on to the next one and the next one, and even in my young mind I thought we were gonna put roofs over them; but we were building the waffle gardens, which is the ancient farming technique of our people. And . . . in my young mind . . . I said "Why build walls without roofs on?" That's when my grandmother said the walls were to prevent the hot wind from drying out the young plants and also retain as much water as they can. On the stories that my grandmother had told me, and even the plan that I did on my work, I even remember being carried on my grandmother's back as a young boy.

Ken Seowtewa, Supai Man, 2010. Oil on canvas, 36 x 46 in.

. . . I used my grandson [as a model] for the young boy being carried by the grandmother. So my mother, Odelle, again helped me with some of the locations where the wells were. . . . I would ask where the old wells were located. So this is what I wanted to do, the basis for my first project with the museum here.

. . . I would like our young people to know that it was a hard life at that time . . . nowadays we just turn on the faucet expecting water to flow through. But imagine during a time of drought . . . not only would our wells and even our river would dry out, we would have springs located within our valley here that people would go over there to get their water. . . . [S]o I want to relate to our children the hard life that our elders had, in a sense fortifying us for our next generation to come . . . now we just have the dry riverbed.

I think it's my Zuni community as a village of artists. . . . [A]s a young kid I was surrounded by art, not just by my family but early artists like Percy Sandy, Salawa Shebola, the Edaakie boys, my grandpa's [Patone Chuyati's] work, Dad's [Alex Seowtewa's] work.

. . . I was taking notes on our Grand Canyon trip that, after each night I laid down and I would jot down my thoughts, my feelings, what I saw, how I felt. So I was jotting down my ideas on a note pad during my whole trip. . . .

[In the Grand Canyon] everything was new to me. Seeing the sights . . . we had such a great camaraderie. You know for the majority of the . . . artists, myself included, to see the actual sites, to be at the canyon the first time was, I think, a life-changing experience for all of us . . . it was really something to see something that we've been told about through stories, through our prayers, and then to actually witness that site itself . . . .

[M]y oldest brother, Octavius . . . he's been on the river trip for, I think, thirteen, fourteen times . . . with . . . religious leaders. . . . [O]n his previous trips, he said he always wondered what that line represented. . . . That line at the bottom pointed from Ribbon Falls, our emergence, to our pueblo of Zuni right here. That simple little line. . . . But, on the last trip that my brother went, he said that where the original line was, somebody was pecking at— defacing—that line on the other side by adding onto it. . . . So even just the artwork that we are creating for the museum here, we're recording how it was actually . . . before the defacement took place.

[T]he primary thing [of Zuni Map Art] is just a visual learning aid for the next generations to come . . . to leave a teaching tool for our next generation.

A:shiwi A:wan Ulohnanne • The Zuni World

Chris Edaakie, Elyes Chasm and Bass, 2010, Digital painting on canvas, 53 x 34.5 in.

Artist Biography
Chris Edaakie

Christopher Edaakie attends the University of New Mexico and is pursuing a degree in graphic arts and diabetes prevention. During his employment at the Zuni Healthy Lifestyles Program, Chris created logos for t-shirts, mugs, and trophies. He was also part of the A:shiwi A:wan Museum and Heritage Center's Grand Canyon exploration to create map art. His painting represents two areas known as Elves Chasm and Bass.

Larson Gasper, Migration of Salt Mother, 2009. Acrylic on canvas, 43 x 33 in.

Artist Statement
Larson Gasper

I've been in the map art project for about two years. . . . [My] first [painting] was . . . Migration of the Salt Mother . . . the second was the Little Colorado River, and the other one . . . [combined] the Little Colorado River, Tanner, and Furnace Flats.

I visited . . . the Colorado River and the Little Colorado . . . sites . . . those [and ancestral] sites [like] Wupatki . . . [are] really unbelievable . . . there's just a kind of a feeling when you get to those sites . . . we do have a relationship to those areas . . . . [T]hat first time I went [to] the Colorado River . . . the beauty and the nature has so much strength in it. . . . How people came out of there, you know. . . . I really was moved.

I think [the map art] . . . shows a lot . . . [to] the non-Zuni . . . or the non-Indians that . . . we [are in] touch with these areas that . . . [for] a lot of [other] people are just more generalized. . . . a lot of these sites . . . even [go] up to Colorado. . . . [Map Art] shows the non-Indians that we do have a lot of connections in these areas.

I saw the aerial . . . photographs [of Zuni Salt Lake] and [heard] the stories . . . from our ancestors—how the Salt Mother left the [Zuni] Village and how [she] migrated, and the story of how she dropped the feather and then the pillars of salt became a rock.

[For my second painting] we went . . . to Flagstaff, and then we went to Wupatki and to Sunset Crater, and [Oak Creek Canyon] . . . you drive through Flagstaff so many times and you don't know that there's anything out there . . . I didn't know there was stuff out there just right off the side of the road. . . . [T]hen there's a connection towards . . . Zuni Heaven . . . after life . . . where our ancestors live . . . that river runs through there and . . . on that picture there's . . . an elderly [Zuni ancestor]. You see petroglyphs everywhere where we go to sites, and you always see the same symbol—there's always a sun symbol. And there's always like a trail—it looks like it is a map or something. . . .

A:shiwi A:wan Ulohnanne • The Zuni World

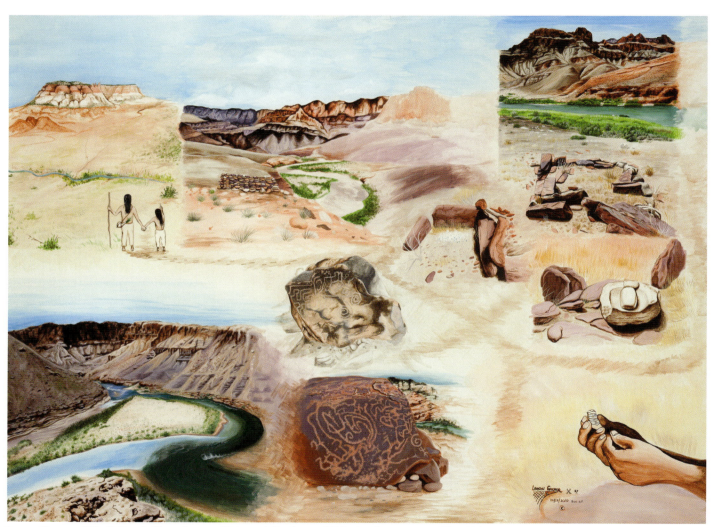

Larson Gasper, Little Colorado River, Furnace Flats, and Cardenas, 2010. Acrylic on canvas, 30 x 40 in.

Larson Gasper, Little Colorado River, 2009. Acrylic on canvas, 40 x 30 in.

[T]here's a lot of art in Zuni, and when you go to school here there's art. . . . I even went to [art] school for maybe a year I was drawn into that . . . I had a feeling for paintings . . . . [But] . . . I haven't touched a paint brush in more than thirteen years. And I came back and . . . it's enjoyable. . . . I amazed myself that I still can paint.

. . . [the painting] was challenging, especially the size of it. . . . I had done some murals before . . . especially landscapes . . . you want to get the effect of . . . the natural colors and your bird's-eye view . . . it is challenging especially when . . . it all comes together, how [a] map comes together. . . . Now I can dust off some of my paints and brushes and finish . . . a bunch of paintings. . . . right now . . . I'm in the commercial printing [business]. . . I've been doing that for about twenty-five years. . . . I run the printing machines . . . . It is like an art work when you're printing, too. So I still have a little connection to that. . . .

The person I really admired . . . when I grew up was Alex Seowtewa . . . the way he tells . . . stories . . . [about] how summer dances all the way towards winter dances. . . . Duane Dishta, he's now another one that really has a good talent, and he does a lot of kachina paintings . . . he has a different taste, designs . . . those are two [artists] . . . from here that really inspired me.

[Among the Map Art advisors]. . . Octavius . . . knows all the sites . . . and he's a medicine man. . . . I got a lot out of him. . . . And some of the guys . . . it was nice to work with them . . . [they gave] input what you need to work on your painting and . . . what you should paint or what you shouldn't . . . there was good positive inputs. . . .

[I]f you see the paintings, everybody has their styles . . . . It was interesting . . . . I admire all these guys. They have a different style and they show it on canvas.

I was telling one of my family members—"You know, I should—since I started doing these landscapes-- those are the things that I . . . avoided when I was growing up but . . . I want to do some more on my own." Especially [because] we have some pretty sites in our reservation . . . I want to try some of those landscape pictures. . . . [T]here's about three or four paintings in my house that I want to finish. Hopefully within a couple of years I'll finish them all.

[The Zuni Map Art Project] was a good experience for me and, hopefully it gets bigger. . . . And a lot of these kids will hopefully take advantage of what we have done and hopefully there's more . . . to be done.

Artist Statement
Elroy Natachu, Jr.

My Grand Canyon] painting generally is based on a village that we encountered after our first rapid. It was right next to Vasey's Paradise, which is a waterfall where they would collect the water that's right near. Then on the third panel, I believe, is a bridge that one of our tour guides pointed out . . . it was an Anasazi bridge high in the cliffs, and then the fourth panel is of Redwall Cavern, which is a very popular landmark within the Grand Canyon. . . .

They show what . . . they had to do to collect the water and where their villages were, how they were built and what was the general location, and that they were always near fresh water. And they would grow crops, not just corn, but . . . any other different kind of food source that they could collect, from cactus to wild berries, and it also showed that the water collection of where they went . . . before and how they collected water in the present time for ritual use at Vasey's Paradise.

[T]he trip was a very enduring trip . . . for the first couple of days it was very cold, and towards maybe about the fourth day it started to heat up and you could start feeling the hot weather and the humidity coming. . . . It was long walks, hot weather, and for me personally, with having only one good—functioning—hand, it was a little tougher, but I managed to pull through and make the whole trip and go to all the sites . . . it was a place that I never really thought I would have a chance to experience, actually going into the canyon and looking at the different landmarks.

I recently started painting in my senior year [at Zuni High School]. I had no more classes to be put into, and I'd been fighting to go into the art program for all three years . . . and finally they let me in on the fourth . . . year.

From that point on I'd never had any experience in any other medium, so this painting would be maybe my third painting. . . . It's acrylic. I wouldn't have had enough time to use oil paints, for it takes too long to dry . . . [but] I prefer oil. Oil paints have a tendency to blend easier and they have more vibrant colors. . . .

A:shiwi A:wan Ulohnanne • The Zuni World

Elroy Natachu, Jr., Tanner, Red Wall Cavern, E:node Bridge, and Vasey's Paradise, 2010. Acrylic on canvas, 48 x 40 in.

[M]y mother and father are silversmiths. They make jewelry. And my sister, she makes . . . fabric dolls that depict . . . different dances [like the] Buffalo Dance. . . . [M]y mother and my sisters . . . would check in and give me different advice on how to maybe do the composition or make [my painting] look more realistic. . . . I like to use more vibrant and bright colors. Many of my uncles, they do paintings . . . one of my cousins, Chris Natachu, he does miniatures that are really tiny and detailed, whereas I like to make big paintings that can be looked at farther away and you can see everything comes together. . . . [I admire] my aunts and my uncles, their works are very detailed and more realistic. That's what I'm really striving to go for is that composition where it actually looks like there's movement within the painting. . . . I think [my painting] plays a part in a new style and also a different way to look at different aspects of Zuni culture.

[The collaboration with advisors] was a good process. It helped me further my understanding of the culture and the different aspects that should be respected, and it just helped to increase my knowledge and also my thought process in how to create certain Zuni Native American artwork.

[Zuni Map Art is] important because it shows Zunis and non-Zunis the importance of different landmarks, but also what happened during our migration stories, or our foundation stories. It gives a better understanding of why we're here, how did we get here, and the different journeys and life lessons from along the way. . . . It's really important to get a better understanding that Zuni's not only known for just the jewelry and fetishes, that we're also great painters. And that each artist here has a different style of painting, whether it be realistic or more abstract work. But from the paintings I think it's really impacting Zuni and other places to where they can actually see different moments in time being depicted, to give them a better understanding instead of just hearing a story and having the listener try and comprehend and visualize the moment in time at which it happened. I think it really helps as a visual medium to really make the stories come alive.

I'm trying to save up my money to where I can go to each site individually and sort of sketch and try and remember the stories that my grandfather and grammy told me about these different places to try and get a better understanding of what they were really trying to teach me—these different lessons.

A:shiwi A:wan Ulohnanne · The Zuni World

Anthony Sanchez, Mesa Verde, 2010. Acrylic on canvas, 40 x 30 in.

Artist Biography
Anthony Sanchez

Anthony Sanchez received a degree in fine arts from the Institute of American Indian Arts. An active painter, Anthony's art is sought by collectors around the world. His brother, Eldred, is also an accomplished painter as well as a woodworker. In the fall of 2010 Anthony completed the painting, Mesa Verde, for this collection.

A:shiwi A:wan Ulohnanne • The Zuni World

Ermalinda Pooacha-Eli, Mesa Verde, 2010. Acrylic with mineral pigments and water collected from Mesa Verde, 30 x 40 in.

Artist Statement
Ermalinda Pooacha-Eli

For Zuni Map Art] I'm painting Mesa Verde. [During the visit to the park] we went on the pathway to go to Spring House and Long House, Balcony House, and saw a lot of the stuff in the museum . . . that was amazing to see how they made ropes out of the yucca, and some of it was hair, too, on the jars. . . . [T]hey had domestic animals, mostly just like dog and then the turkeys they would use the down feathers . . . to make blankets . . . and there was a lot of pottery that . . . they would make and all the plants that they used to make dye then and to eat. The different types of vegetation that we were looking at was the wild potatoes, the tomatillos, and different berries, and the cactus fruit.

The map art project . . . shows different sites that the Zunis are connected to, which I didn't know was Chaco Canyon and Mesa Verde. I mean, there's so many and just with all these artists portraying the sites and all it's like a story, where we migrated from and what the people are all about; and with the artists coming together to do this collaboration, I think it's a great idea. I'm still learning. So it's a learning process—ongoing process . . . it gives a lot of the local artists a chance to . . . showcase their work. But, above it all, it's like mainly for the community . . . the Zunis, so it's never too late to learn . . . about our culture.

[I]t gives me a chance to show people my style of artwork because everyone has their own style. I'm gonna go ahead and include some of . . . the clay and the sand and the plants—incorporate that into the painting itself.

The clay is from Mesa Verde itself. We were allowed to . . . take a few things. So . . . I went in and uprooted some potato plants and tomatillos. And the clay . . . I . . . pounded it out and sifted it, and then made my paint mixture out of it—the clay itself—and put it on the canvas.

The prayers that they had a long time ago and prayers of today . . . we all still . . . thank Mother Earth, and I thank the ancestors for giving me this gift in art and . . . that's just something in me to say . . . "Thank you very [much for] giving me this talent so I can at least teach other people and show other people through artwork" . . . what we're about as far as . . . Zunis . . . A:shiwi . . . and how we are as a community. Because Mesa Verde, you know . . . they were a community of pottery makers, masonry workers, bakers, cooks.

[Working with the advisors] was very touching, too, because they would take us to the sites, mainly the springs where . . . we would do our offerings to the spirits and . . . you could sense that . . . they were there and that they were happy to see us there. I would just look at the walls and look in amazement at how it used to be a long time ago and try to imagine what it was like, you know, with babies crawling around, dogs barking. The same thing that happens over here but just a long time ago . . . looking at the walls and their designs on the walls, their handprints. . . .

With the advisors saying their blessings . . . it was very touching, and I know we were blessed on that trip . . . every night I would go to the room and just take in everything that I had seen that day and it's like "Wow, this is so surreal," and just to imagine being there and . . . thanking our ancestors. . . . I'm glad Octavius [Seowtewa] was there to explain certain things to us. He was saying that perhaps they did it this way, and the reason why. But, as a woman, and trying to portray the side of Mesa Verde in my own eyes as a woman . . . it's gonna be different from what these guys have portrayed.

My mentor was Grandpa Alex Seowtewa . . . he was a lot of influence on me as far as growing up. . . . I grew up with Grandpa Alex, dancing with him and with his artwork.

[For Zuni Map Art] what would be interesting is if they have the younger generation—the school students—start their own little map project and see it from the kids' point of view and how they see it and have them paint, you know, the Grand Canyon, Mesa Verde. . . . It could go with the little kids and encourage them where the kids looking at the other kids' map art, that "Oh, if they can draw like that, maybe I can, too" and then . . . go from there . . . after this map project is over with, while it's still ongoing, they'll be the next generation—the little ones—to keep it going.

Artist Statement
Alex Seowtewa

My painting for the Zuni Map Art will be at] Chaco Canyon. In Zuni we call that place in our language Heshoda Bit'tsule'a. If I interpret the English, "Round House".... I know that they have names to certain sections of this historic place, but I have in mind to capture the Fajada Butte.... I have witnessed it from the distance. That one time I was up there with a Zuni [high school] history class.... I ... orally interpreted the historic site with the students, with their history teacher.

[My father, Patone Chuyati] he did see a few illustrations that I did in my early years when I was a little kid . . . sometimes he could sit down with me and we could just . . . use the outside beehive [oven] charcoal. . . . I began to realize and understood that my late father is an artist, and he used to interpret a lot of this early rock art with me . . . He interpreted to me certain spiral readings, humanistic form figures with tails, describing these figures as prehistoric, that used to live in the caves. And one time . . . we came across . . . this smaller spiral reading, pictoglyph, and he interpreted . . . his . . . grand uncle was a Sun Priest—in Zuni, Pekwin. What his late uncle interpreted to him . . . [they witnessed] that spiral reading . . . to calculate the season of Zuni religious calendar. . . . How in the heck [could] this have happened? They didn't have computers like now we deal with, but scientifically, and I listened in to my father's interpretation, so what my creative mind registered right now, and this is just below the . . . Fajada Butte area. I would interpret it as kind of a little aged Sun Priest . . . not in the full customary clothing but just the regular ordinary clothing, looking at Fajada.

So my own father interpreted a lot of these important cycles . . . and I listened and I asked questions . . . and that was just a terrific interpretation that the last surviving Sun Priest that I used to witness had died in early 1950s when I was in my adolescent age because my late father—grandfather—maternal grandfather was a first Rain Priest to the North—Ka:kwe Mossi—and this last surviving Rain Priest in Zuni—he was known as Nab'Billie, but religiously he was known as Pekwin, the Sun Priest. And he used to visit my late grandfather, my mother's father.

I feel honored now to be part of this team [Zuni Map Art] —just a little fraction of it. The other great young artists are taking the full advantage of this good, good project. I support it more than one hundred percent . . . [the Zuni community will] benefit because orally we have to interpret to our present generation so they'll grow up to know their identity, what richness we were blessed for so many centuries. . . . I think to this type of project as it expands into other native areas or ethnic areas, it will give them a good lesson, and they could really adopt this . . . as a spearhead project. If we could just apply this to the whole world, we'll come back to our common sense to live with peace and harmony.

. . . I could reflect it to my ancestors' roots—the dwellers, centuries ago, that lived at Chaco Canyon, Mesa Verde, Village of Great Kivas nearby eight miles from here. They practiced patience. If you see their chunking walls, smaller rocks with primitive walls, they built this from the foundation. Rooms were small. When I look at that idea of their dwellings, Chaco Canyon, Mesa Verde, you name it, that's a lesson in front of me . . . If I want to do art, I could just record, go over my little computer upstairs of thinking and come across something that I haven't done and I just put it on a canvas or illustration board. . . . I don't take my sketchbook around with me to do the sketching . . . I just study something so solid and there it is. This is what I emphasize to a lot of promising artists . . . sometimes I do rework on my art if it doesn't come but I don't intend to pressure myself because emotions are important to our minds. . . . I have the great role models that left me a history . . . our ancient artists'. . . . rock art. It'd probably take time for them to create something on the rock. They have to study the surface, the color tone, so their expression of whatever they come up from their mind will go on this rock.

My maternal grandfather's teaching, his . . . strong philosophy, is that life is a gift. Never be critical, respect your life, fulfill your life. Death is part of living. My maternal grandfather, my grandmother, they both were over a hundred when my mother died, so I was much closer to listening in to their teachings. . . . I want to give a credibility to my grandparents . . . they taught me a lot of words of wisdom.

I always liked the feel of art, I guess from a small kid growing up, kind of like my late father, when I used to help him. He could just sketch, but he never taught me as an art teacher even though he could form a lot of things. But I could do that here and there as I went to school, and I just only put two semesters on art scholarship. . . . I was given this honorary doctorate degree in humanities, not from my state here in New Mexico, but at Nashua, New Hampshire—Daniel Webster College back in May 15, 1999. And I was born in 1933.

Alex Seowtewa and son Octavius discuss a concept for Alex's Chaco Canyon painting. Photograph by Jim Enote.

Acknowledgments

There was never any question that from its home at the A:shiwi A:wan Museum and Heritage Center this collection would travel to the Museum of Northern Arizona. It is fitting that the MNA should undertake this exhibition of Zuni map art. While the MNA is recognized as an exemplary institution with magnificent Zuni collections, it is also appreciated as a place that accommodates Zuni ideas and expressions. Dr. Robert Breunig's encouragement and support as Director of the MNA has facilitated the introduction of A:shiwi A:wan Ulohnanne - The Zuni World to an audience eager to learn from an unfamiliar perspective of the Colorado Plateau.

Among many people we must thank are the Zuni map art advisors Norman Cooeyate, Valerie Epaloose, Wilfred Eriacho, Odell Jaramillo, Quentin Lalio, Jed Peynetsa, Veronica Peynetsa, Arlen Quetawki, Octavius Seowtewa, Dan Simplicio, Edward Wemytewa, and Willard Zunie who gave generously of their time to help guide the Zuni Map Art movement to where it is now.

Dr. Jennifer McLerran's exceptional knowledge and personal devotion to the study of Zuni art has been essential to putting this catalog together. Her interviews with the artists in the collection and her essay make an important contribution to the study and enjoyment of Zuni art.

Finally, we are especially grateful to the Annenberg Foundation, Christensen Fund, Lannan Foundation, and National Geographic Society Expeditions Council for their generous support to help create this exceptional exposition of Zuni art and exploration.

Elahkwa (Thank you)

Jim Enote, Curator A:shiwi A:wan Ulohnanne – The Zuni World
and Director, A:shiwi A:wan Museum and Heritage Center

I would like to thank all of the Zuni map artists who so generously shared their time, their stories and their art with me. I am also enormously grateful to Octavius Seowtewa for his generosity and patience and Curtis Quam and Kathy Farretta for their invaluable assistance.

Jim Enote is a tremendous leader who was entirely devoted to the integrity and success of this project, and I wish to thank him for all he did. Editor Rose Houk and designer Julie Sullivan were wonderful partners who worked tirelessly to create a beautiful, high-quality publication.

Jennifer McLerran
Co-editor, A:shiwi A:wan Ulohnanne – The Zuni World
Assistant Professor, Art History
Northern Arizona University